OVERCOMING SHYNESS AND SOCIAL PHOBIA

D1507589

A JASON ARONSON BOOK

ROWMAN & LITTLEFIELD PUBLISHERS, INC.
Lanham • Boulder • New York • Toronto • Oxford

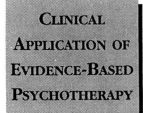

CLINICAL APPLICATION OF EVIDENCE-BASED PSYCHOTHERAPY

A Series of Books Edited By
William C. Sanderson

In response to the demands of the new health care environment, there is a movement in psychology (and in all of health care) toward defining empirically supported treatment approaches (i.e., treatments that have been shown to be effective in controlled research studies). The future demands of psychotherapy are becoming clear. In response to pressures from managed care organizations and various practice guidelines, clinicians will be required to implement evidence-based, symptom-focused treatments.

Fortunately, such treatments exist for a variety of the most commonly encountered disorders. However, it has been extremely difficult to disseminate these treatments from clinical research centers, where the treatments are typically developed, to practitioners. More often than not, the level of detail in treatment protocols used in research studies is insufficient to teach a clinician to implement the treatment.

This series, *Clinical Application of Evidence-Based Psychotherapy*, will address this issue. For each disorder covered, empirically supported psychological procedures will be identified. Then, an intensive, step-by-step, session-by-session treatment application will be provided. A detailed clinical vignette will be woven throughout, including session transcripts.

All books in this series are written by experienced clinicians who have applied the treatments to a wide variety of patients, and have supervised and taught other clinicians how to apply them.

Social Phobia:
Clinical Application of Evidence-Based Psychotherapy
Ronald Rapee and William C. Sanderson

Overcoming Shyness and Social Phobia:
A Step-by-Step Guide
Ronald Rapee

Specific Phobias:
Clinical Applications of Evidence-Based Psychotherapy
Timothy J. Bruce and William C. Sanderson

Cognitive-Behavioral Treatment of Depression
Janet S. Klosko and William C. Sanderson

OVERCOMING SHYNESS

and

SOCIAL PHOBIA

A STEP-BY-STEP GUIDE

Ronald M. Rapee, Ph.D.

A JASON ARONSON BOOK

ROWMAN & LITTLEFIELD PUBLISHERS, INC.

Published in the United States of America
by Rowman & Littlefield Publishers, Inc.
A wholly owned subsidiary of The Rowman & Littlefield Publishing Group, Inc.
4501 Forbes Boulevard, Suite 200, Lanham, Maryland 20706
www.rowmanlittlefield.com

PO Box 317
Oxford
OX2 9RU, UK

British Library Cataloguing in Publication Information Available

Library of Congress Cataloging-in-Publication Data

Rapee, Ronald M.
  Overcoming shyness and social phobia : a step-by-step guide / by Ronald M. Rapee.
    p. cm.
  Includes bibliographical references and index.
  ISBN: 978-0-7657-0120-6
  1. Bashfulness. 2. Anxiety. 3. Social phobia—Treatment. I. Title.
BF575.B3R36 1998
155.2'32—dc21   97-27509

Printed in the United States of America

⊖™ The paper used in this publication meets the minimum requirements of American
National Standard for Information Sciences—Permanence of Paper for Printed Library
Materials, ANSI/NISO Z39.48-1992.

To Wendy

My partner in life

CONTENTS

Introduction ix

Lesson 1 Motivation and Self Control 1

Lesson 2 Understanding Shyness 11
and Social Phobia

Lesson 3 Thinking Realistically—I 23

Lesson 4 Thinking Realistically—II 39

Lesson 5 Training Your Attention 53

Lesson 6 Reality Testing 63

Lesson 7 Getting Feedback and Improving 79
Performance

Lesson 8 Taking Stock 91

Lesson 9 Special Topics 97

Conclusion and a Word about Drugs 115
and Alcohol

Index 117

INTRODUCTION

Everyone who knew her knew that Jan was a little quiet. But they also knew her as a competent and intelligent businesswoman, an efficient mother of two great kids, and a wonderful friend. What very few of them knew was that life was often a struggle for Jan, a struggle of doubts, uncertainties, and insecurity. Whenever she had to present a trophy at sports night, or make a business presentation, or simply talk in front of the parents' group, her head would spin, her heart would pound, and she would be covered in sweat. Jan did not think that she came across well, but rather believed that others thought that she was inadequate, inefficient, and sometimes even stupid. Sometimes she would make up excuses so that she could get out of parties or dinner engagements because she couldn't cope with the mental effort involved in preparing herself to go. And sometimes, even though she felt very guilty, Jan would have a glass of brandy to settle her nerves before she went out to meet new people.

Jan is typical of a large number of people whose lives are affected by their worries about what other people think of them. Some, like Jan, present a picture of quiet confidence to the outside world, while inside they are terrified. For others, their shyness is painfully obvious to everyone.

If you are reading this book, then the chances are that worries about what other people think of you has affected your life in some way. There may be obvious effects, like having too few friends, or being too scared to talk to that boy or girl that you like. Or there may be more subtle effects, like missing the opportunity to join an important committee, or not daring to wear that shirt that looks so good on someone else. Whatever the effects, if you think that your life is being limited by social anxiety, then you can, and should, do something about it. Reading this book is the first step. Putting into practice the techniques and strategies that we discuss is the next one. Applying these steps rigorously may not be easy, but with hard work and regular practice, you will find your life turning around.

The techniques and strategies discussed in this book are based on the most up-to-date studies in the world. These same techniques are used in several international research programs with very high levels of success. One of the main things you will notice is that they are not magical or mysterious secrets. Rather, they are practical, commonsense strategies that are aimed at teaching you new ways of controlling and managing your shyness. Many of the techniques will be methods that you may have heard of before or may even have tried yourself. Maybe they have worked to some extent for you in the past. Whether they have or have not, the difference is that here they are presented as a comprehensive package. In addition, in order to make them work, you have to be committed to practice hard and often so that the strategies become second nature to you.

WHAT IS SHYNESS?

We all know what a shy person looks like. He's the one in the corner of the room, talking to no one, blushing furiously, and staring at the floor—right? Wrong? There is no doubt that some shy people look like this. But what about the loudmouth who won't stop butting into the meeting and forcing all his opinions on everyone and when you talk to him later he looks sheepish and says, "Oh, I always get a little too talkative when I'm feeling embarrassed."

Shyness shows itself in different ways in different people. We will talk more about exactly what it is later, but briefly, *being shy means*

being nervous or worried about what other people are thinking of you.
It usually also involves being frightened of and avoiding activities or situations where you might become the center of people's attention. However, the situations and events that people fear are specific to every individual.

Shyness can refer to particular situations ("I get shy when I have to sing in front of people"), or to a certain person across situations ("He is generally such a shy person"). Many words and terms have been used to describe shyness, including social phobia, social anxiety, avoidant personality disorder, dating anxiety, heterosocial anxiety, to name a few. Some phrases, such as social phobia and avoidant personality disorder, are professional terms while others are more common. With minor exceptions, they all refer basically to the same thing. In this book we will use the words *shyness*, *social phobia*, and *social anxiety*, but you should use whatever term feels most comfortable.

FOUR CASES

Before we go any further, I would like to introduce you to four people who will become very important in helping you to learn the techniques in this book. All of them can be described as shy or socially phobic but they differ in the degree of shyness they have and in the way in which shyness affects their lives.

Throughout this book we will return to these four people and use their problems to help show how the various treatment strategies can be applied. You may want to read through these cases several times to remind yourself of the many ways in which social anxiety can show itself. You may also want to pick the person who is most like you. Think about how he or she is similar to or different from you.

Adam

Adam is 27 years old and works as a sales representative for a computer software company. He is married with one child and enjoys playing golf on the weekends.

Adam's main difficulty is that he shakes uncontrollably whenever he feels that he is the center of attention. Many situations make him feel this way, but Adam's two most difficult situations are drinking or writing in front of other people. Whenever Adam has to write something (such as sign a check or fill out a form) and there are other people nearby, he becomes very anxious and worries that he is going to begin to shake and will then not be able to write properly. Similarly, when he has a cup of coffee or a beer in a bar with other people around, he worries that he will shake and spill the drink, causing people to laugh at him.

As a result of these fears, Adam avoids almost all situations where he might have to drink with others or write in front of them. For example, he has been having a great deal of difficulty in his work because many of the sales secured by other salespeople are made over a drink with clients. As a result, he often seems unfriendly because he refuses offers of coffee or invitations to lunch. In addition, it is hard for him to sign the necessary paperwork to close a sale. He often makes awkward excuses and signs things in the car when no one is around. Lately, Adam has begun to look for other work.

Aside from work, Adam's golf is not as much fun as it used to be because he never joins his friends for an after-game drink and they are beginning to lose interest in him.

Similarly, Adam tries to get out of going to social events or will often leave before the eating and drinking begin. As a result, his wife is becoming depressed and there are quite a few arguments. He has never had a credit card because of the fear of signing his name in front of salespeople.

Adam says he has always been a little shy but the real fears seemed to start around five years ago following a particularly heavy night of partying. The next day, Adam went for a job interview and was feeling so shaky from the night before that he spilled a cup of coffee all over his potential boss. Needless to say, he did not get the job and his confidence took quite a battering.

Jenny

Jenny is a 33-year-old woman who looks after her family comprised of her husband Jim and three boys. Jenny says that as long as she can remember she has been quiet and lacking in confidence. Other people have always described her as shy. She married Jim, her only boyfriend, twelve years ago and they tend to lead a quiet life, centering mainly around the family. Jenny worked only briefly in her life and didn't really enjoy it, largely because she was always worried that the boss would ask her to do something she couldn't handle or that she would make a mistake. She has always had a small circle of friends but has found it harder to keep in touch as her family has grown. Jenny volunteers for the school canteen, helps out with the children's sports groups, and goes along to Jim's business dinners. However, she rarely feels comfortable in these situations, especially when she doesn't know everybody there. She generally feels best when she is at home.

Jenny is basically happy with her life and is grateful for what she has. But she can't help thinking that it would be nice to have a little more confidence to make some new friends, start a job and career, and be a little more daring in the clothes she wears and the people she talks to.

Heather

Heather is a 48-year-old woman whose husband of eighteen years recently left her. Heather has always been shy and anxious and recalls a particularly awkward adolescence. She remembers being 18, having few friends, and being painfully shy with boys. She never went to school dances, rarely went out at night, tried to avoid looking people in the eye, and hardly ever spoke to people unless she knew them well. Since these early days, Heather's confidence has grown a little as she matured, but she has always found it difficult to be in any kind of social situation. Heather believes that she looks awkward and unattractive and whenever the conversation turns to her, she immediately feels that people will think she is stupid. She avoids parties and dinners whenever she can and rarely starts conversations. She always tries to fit in with others and even avoids walking around in crowded places because she thinks everyone is watching her. Many of the friends and social interactions that Heather previously had were from her husband's contacts.

Heather's unassertiveness meant that her husband always called the shots in their marriage. Nevertheless, she generally preferred to be with him. Since he left a few months ago, Heather has lost even more confidence and has become quite depressed. She is suddenly forced to find a job and make her own friends.

George

George is 38 and a night watchman for a large chemical plant. Although he would like to find a partner, George has had very few opportunities to meet women and has only once in his life had a brief romantic relationship. Generally, George is so frightened of being hurt by others that he never allows himself to become involved in a relationship unless he is absolutely certain that he will be liked. As a result, he has no close friends and is often lonely.

George is very worried about what other people think of him. He almost always believes that people are judging him and that they think him stupid and unpleasant. This is the case whether he is actually talking to these people or is simply physically close to them. As a result, he tries to avoid almost all contact with other people. He shops early in the morning, he never socializes, and he avoids making inquiries or talking to people in general. George actually tries to make himself invisible by not looking at people, dressing in dull, unremarkable colors, and standing at the back in groups. In fact, he has chosen to work as a night watchman for the past eleven years specifically to avoid major responsibilities and interaction with people at work. When he does have to meet a new person, even if it is only someone coming to repair the TV, he will often have a few glasses of beer to help him get through it. Because of this "self medication," George actually became quite dependent on alcohol a few years ago. Although he is now able to manage the amount he consumes, alcohol dependency is still a constant danger.

Meeting these four people, Adam, Heather, Jenny, and George, might help to give you a better understanding of some of the many and varied aspects of social anxiety. These four people all share the same basic characteristic: a fear of what other people think of them. Yet they show some of the many different ways in which this fear can affect people's lives.

HOW TO USE THIS BOOK

If you think that shyness is affecting your life in any way, then this book can teach you the techniques and strategies to help you overcome your fears. But it is important to remember that the book itself will not magically take away your fear. Only *you* have the power to do that by carefully and conscientiously practicing the techniques we discuss.

It is certainly possible to take yourself through the procedures in this book and to learn to be your own "therapist." But, let's face it—most of us don't have the willpower to keep ourselves completely on track without some help. In addition, it is often hard to understand exactly how to apply something described in a book to our own lives. Therefore, I strongly recommend that if you are serious about working this program, you should find a competent therapist to help you apply it to your specific circumstances. When you see a therapist, you should not be afraid to ask about his or her qualifications, training, and experience in dealing with your type of problems. This might be hard for you to do, but it is important if you want to get the best help. If it is too hard to ask these questions in person, you should be able to get this information over the phone. In addition, you should show the therapist this book (if s/he did not give it to you) and check that s/he is happy to go along with this type of approach. A companion therapist guide to this program is available (R. M. Rapee and W. C. Sanderson, *Social Phobia: Clinical Application of Evidence-*

Based Psychotherapy, Northvale, NJ: Jason Aronson, 1998) which will guide your therapist in helping you to understand and apply the techniques described in this book.

While many of these techniques are general anxiety management strategies, it should be remembered that this program is specifically aimed at managing social anxieties. Often, people with social anxiety have additional problems. Some of the more common ones include feeling depressed, being dependent on drugs or alcohol, or having other forms of anxiety, such as panic attacks or phobias. In some cases, learning to control your social anxiety will help to minimize these other problems. However, it may be that you will need more specific programs to help you to manage these other problems. This is all the more reason to make sure you are seeing a qualified mental health practitioner who should be able to guide you through these other problems.

So, now that these preliminaries are out of the way, let's begin the program to help you control your shyness.

1

MOTIVATION
AND
SELF CONTROL

As we discussed in the introduction, *the main key to success is practice*. The techniques we will cover are not magic. They do not work like a pill that you simply swallow with a glass of water. They are *skills* that have to be *learned* and have to become part of your usual way of living. Just as you have to practice to become good at the piano or to learn to type, so too you have to practice, practice, practice the techniques in this program.

If you are like me, then you are probably not too good at doing unpleasant things like practicing techniques. Motivation, then, is going to be an important part of the program. If you can keep up your motivation to change, then practicing will follow. If your motivation drops, it will be a real battle to practice.

You will probably find that throughout the program your motivation and enthusiasm will come and go. When you have a success (and I hope there will be many), your motivation will skyrocket. However, when you have a failure (and no doubt there will be some), your motivation will drop. This is where a therapist can really help. However, there are also some things you can do to increase the chances of keeping your motivation up. Let's explore them now.

THE WHYS OF CHANGE

On the next page, there is space for you to write down two types of things. First, I want you to think carefully about your current life and the role that shyness plays in it. Try to think about the obvious things, such as jobs you may have avoided, and the subtle things, ways you cut your hair, for example. Then make a list of some of the most important ways that shyness has limited and interfered with your life.

Next, think about the future, an ideal future in which you have successfully mastered your shyness. Try to imagine what life would be like without shyness, what you would be like as a non-shy person. Write down a description of yourself and, in particular, how your life will be different when you are less shy.

Keep thinking about these issues and keep adding to these lists whenever you can (see Table 1–1). Then, when you find your motivation dropping, get out the lists and use them to remind yourself of why you started this program. Perhaps you can even keep the lists next to your bed so that you regularly remind yourself of the reasons for wanting to change.

SELF CONTROL

Self control is a popular term that is used to refer to all sorts of personal characteristics. In psychology we use it to refer to a number of procedures by which we increase the chances of doing what we are supposed to do at the right time. Sounds good, doesn't it?

Basically, the idea is that when you are feeling enthused and motivated (like now, at the beginning of the program), you organize your life so that some of the less pleasant things (such as having to practice a tedious technique) are fixed in place. That way, if your motivation drops at some later point, you are already committed and it is hard to get out of your practice. Let me give you an example.

Social fears limit my life by ...	If I was not socially anxious, I would be able to ...
Table 1–1. Form for recording limitations of social anxiety and benefits of improvement	

Assume that you want to learn to play the piano which, of course, involves a whole lot of practice. When you begin, you are probably feeling very motivated. Take the opportunity, then, to lock yourself in. For example, you might prepay your first ten lessons. In addition, you might promise to give your friends a recital in two months. Or you might schedule your first piano exam in two months' time. By committing yourself to these things now, when you are feeling motivated, you are making it very hard to avoid practice at a later time when perhaps your motivation is not quite as strong.

Self-control techniques like this generally fall into two groups: financial and social. Financial strategies involve making a financial commitment based on your practice. For example, if you want to make sure that you go for a jog every day this week, you might decide to put $5 into a jar every time you jog. Then at the end of the week, you can take the money and buy yourself something nice. Of course, this way the more you jog, the more money you have to spend on the present you give yourself.

Alternately, you can use a punishment method. You might decide to put $10 into a jar every time you do *not* go for your jog. Then, at the end of the week, you should donate the money in the jar to your least-liked charity! Of course financial self-control techniques like this only work to the extent to which you are honest with yourself. It is easy to cheat. Social techniques or a combination of social and financial techniques are often better.

With social self-control techniques, the idea is to include someone else into your commitment. Let's continue with our jogging example. When you are feeling very enthusiastic, you might find a friend who is also keen to go jogging and the two of you might plan to go for a regular run. That way, if one of you doesn't feel like jogging, the other one can do the encouraging. Similarly, you might plan to meet each other every day at a particular place. That way, you actually have to turn up because you know your partner is waiting for you.

Finally, you can combine financial and social self-control techniques, which is often the most effective way to go. For example, you might give a friend $70 at the beginning of the week and ask her to pay you back $10 every time you jog. If there is money left at the end of seven days, your friend can spend it on whatever she wishes.

Paying yourself money, making bargains with friends—you may be thinking that all of this sounds a little childish and silly. However, research has shown that self-control procedures like these can make a big difference to the amount of practice that people do. Obviously, it is easy to cheat or to give up. But if you give it serious effort, then it does work. Generally, most people find that one or the other technique is best for them. Try to experiment a bit and see which one works best for you.

RECORDING YOUR PROGRESS

One of the most important parts of the change process is learning to become an observer of your own behavior. In other words, you will need to observe yourself and the way you think and act almost as if you were an outsider looking in.

Why Keep Records?

Keeping good, up-to-date records can be very useful for four main reasons:

1. *Helping motivation:* As we discussed in the last section, keeping your motivation high will be an important part of getting through this program. By keeping records of your progress and your practice, you can help to give yourself a push when the going gets tough. If you have a setback, you can get out your records and remind yourself of how much you have changed since you began.

2. *Learning skills:* Each of the techniques we will be covering in this program involves learning new and sometimes difficult skills. By keeping detailed records, you can help to break down the techniques and see where problems as well as benefits come from. This will make it much easier to learn these skills and apply them to your life.

3. *Identifying all your fears:* Obviously you have a good idea of what sorts of things make you anxious. But sometimes you may be worried about things that are less easy to identify. Keeping records, especially the one we will discuss shortly, will help you to identify situations that you may never have realized were part of your fear. Being honest with yourself and identifying all of the situations that make you feel anxious will be very important if you want to achieve maximum change.

4. *Becoming more objective:* One of the hardest things we all have to do if we want to change is to learn to see ourselves *truly* as others see us. If you are socially anxious, seeing yourself objectively is a particular problem. By keeping and reflecting on records of your thoughts, feelings, and actions, you can start to become more realistic in the way you see yourself. This may mean uncovering some more problems, but it also involves recognizing good things. Record keeping is a helpful tool for seeing yourself realistically, which is the first step toward changing your behavior.

Throughout this program you will need to keep detailed and accurate records of a number of different things if you want to get the most out of each technique. Forms to help you record will be described at the appropriate times. However, the first step of change involves learning to observe yourself the way you are *now*. To help you do this, I will now describe a form to record your thoughts, feelings, and behaviors.

Social Situations Record

The first form to keep is a record of the situations and events that make you feel anxious. For each situation you will need to record your thoughts, feelings, and reactions.

You will see a copy of the Social Situations Record on the next page (Table 1–2). You should carry it with you for the next two weeks. In fact, if you are doing it properly, you will need to make lots of copies. Every time you feel anxious, or very soon after, no matter how little, take the form out and write down the details. In the first column, record the situation or event that caused the anxiety. Note that this may not always be a current event but might be simply when you think about an upcoming event. In the next column, record what you were thinking about the situation or event (in other words, your worries). Next, at the top of the form, there is a scale that goes from 0 to 8. Zero refers to no anxiety at all, and 8 is the worst terror you can imagine. Use the numbers on this scale to indicate your degree of nervousness or shyness in the third column. Finally, the last two columns are for you to record your reaction to the event. In column 4, record your physical reaction. For example, your heart may have raced or you may have blushed. In column 5 record any avoidance behaviors. For example, you may have tried to get away, or you may have moved toward the back of a group.

To help make this form a little clearer, I have put in an example as completed by Heather, one of the people I described in the first chapter (see Table 1–3).

Degree of nervousness or shyness

0	1	2	3	4	5	6	7	8
none		slight		moderate		quite a bit		extreme

Table 1–2. Social Situations Record

Situation or Event	Negative Thoughts or Worries	Anxiety/Shyness (0–8)	Physical Reaction	Avoidance or Other Behaviors

Degree of nervousness or shyness

0	1	2	3	4	5	6	7	8
none		slight		moderate		quite a bit		extreme

Table 1–3. Part of Heather's sample Social Situations Record

Situation or Event	Negative Thoughts or Worries	Anxiety/Shyness (0–8)	Physical Reaction	Avoidance or Other Behaviors
Shopping at local supermarket	I look really weird	5	Tense, shaking	Didn't look at anyone, hurried
Small talk with neighbor	I wonder if she likes me	3	A little hot	Spoke a little fast
Job interview	They will think I'm stupid I'll never get this job I sound so pathetic	8	Blushing, sweating, tense, pounding heart, dry mouth	Spoke fast, hardly smiled, didn't elaborate on answers
Walking to bus from interview	Everyone can see how hopeless I am	4	Tense, nauseous, headachy	Eyes to ground, rushed home quickly

It is best if you keep using this form for at least the next two weeks. You may decide that it is so useful that you want to keep using it. That's great. But if not, at least try to go for two weeks to get a good spread of different events and situations. I suggest that you don't go on to the next lesson until you have used this form for at least a week, but two weeks is better.

ABOUT TASKS

At the end of each lesson I will include one or more tasks to be done before moving on to the next lesson. These tasks usually involve putting the lesson into practice. It is essential that you do these assignments fully if you want to improve. Remember, the key to managing your shyness is practice! I will also include a checklist of all the tasks from previous lessons. That way you will always be clear as to the practice you should be doing between lessons.

SUMMARY

In this lesson I introduced the concepts of motivation and recording.

- Motivation can be maintained by using self-control techniques.

- There are two main types of self-control techniques: financial and social.

- To aid motivation, it is also very useful to complete lists of why you want to change and how your life would be different without shyness.

- Recording is important for four main reasons: helping motivation, learning skills, identifying all your fears, and becoming more objective.

10

TASKS AND CHECKLIST

✓ Write out your lists of how social fears limit your life and how life would be different without shyness. Put these lists someplace where you will see them regularly.

✓ Think about what types of self-control techniques you might be able to use while you are working this program and take steps to put them into action. For example, discuss with a friend the possibility of working the program together or prepare a money jar for your rewards and incentives.

✓ Use the Social Situations Record to record any episodes of social anxiety for at least the next two weeks.

LESSON 2

UNDERSTANDING SHYNESS AND SOCIAL PHOBIA

One of the most common questions asked by people whose lives are affected by shyness is "Why am I like this?" The answer, obviously, is a complex one. In short, we are not entirely sure. Research into understanding more about social anxiety is continuing all the time. However, we do have a number of answers—enough to give us a pretty good guide.

FACTS AND FIGURES

How Many People Are Shy?

The number of people who report social anxiety is a constantly changing figure, depending on your definition. As you saw from our four cases, the range of people who call themselves shy or socially phobic is very broad. There do exist some accepted definitions, and figures change depending on which is used. According to the most widely accepted psychiatric definition of social phobia, up to 13 percent of the population in Western countries fits into this category. On the other hand, studies that have asked people, "Do you have a problem with shyness?" find up to 40 percent of the population answers "yes." So, as you can see, you are certainly not alone!

Men or Women?

The sex ratio for social phobia is also a complex issue, depending on the sample of people surveyed.

The most common figures are from clinical populations, that is, those people who go to a mental health professional or clinic for treatment. In this group of people, we usually find around equal numbers of men and women, possibly even slightly more men with social phobia.

On the other hand, when studies of the general population are done—for example, when university students are surveyed with a questionnaire or random people in households are interviewed—we generally find more women than men who seem to be socially anxious (approximately 60 percent–70 percent women).

How do we arrive at these numbers? Well, the most logical explanation is that women are somewhat more likely to be shy than men. However, in current Western societies, where the social pressure is often more on men to perform and lead (being aggressive at work, being the initiator on a date, and so on), men's lives may be more affected by shyness and so they are more likely to seek help. If this is so, we should see more women coming to therapists for help with social anxiety in the coming years as the social roles of men and women change.

Once Shy, Always Shy?

What happens to shy people as they get older? Does shyness come and go, or is it a constant throughout one's life? These are questions to which we don't know all the answers yet, but it certainly seems that shyness usually doesn't disappear by itself. No doubt there are exceptions and we have all heard stories about shy, retiring kids who became confident, outgoing adults. In addition, most of us generally become a little more confident as we grow older. But in general, people who are shy at a young age are usually still shy many years later. There may be slight ups and downs, depending on what is happening in someone's life, but by and large, shyness usually has a habit of staying around. Of course, that does not mean that you can't learn to overcome shyness by working at it!

CAUSES OF SHYNESS

So why do people become shy? Again, that's something we don't know very much about, but we do have enough information to construct some plausible theories.

The first thing to point out is that people are not either shy or not shy. Just like people's height or weight or hair color, it is something that goes from not at all shy to extremely shy. People vary in their degree of shyness right through the range.

Second, shyness is not the same for all people. One person may be terrified of signing a check in front of someone and yet be quite happy to give a speech to an audience of 500. To another person, giving a talk, even to ten people, might be the stuff of their worst nightmares, but they may not give a second thought to signing a check.

Based on these two points, it seems logical to assume that like height, weight, and so on, your basic level of shyness is likely to be partly based on your genetic makeup. However, the specifics of your shyness, the individual fears and worries, are very likely to have been shaped by the environment in which you grew up.

Our Genes

So where is the "shyness gene"? All of the information we have so far suggests that there is no specific gene that directly determines how shy we are. Rather, it seems that there is a gene or genes that control the degree to which people are generally emotional. This is likely to cover an entire range. Some people are very emotional, some are hardly emotional, and the rest vary in between. Most shy people probably fall at the upper end of emotionality. This means that they are likely not only to be shy, but they may also be worriers, become depressed, have panic attacks, and so on. However, there is also a plus side. Emotional people are more likely to be kind-hearted, conscientious, and trustworthy. In other words, the degree of emotionality you have is part of you and it has both good and bad aspects to it. It is part of what makes you unique.

All of this means that there are limits to the changes you can make. To understand this better, think of your weight. You can change your weight to some extent by proper diet and exercise. But it is very hard (some would say impossible) to change your basic body structure or become a totally different-looking person. In the same way, while you can learn to manage your shyness so that it no longer interferes with your life, you cannot (nor should you want to) completely change your basic emotionality. If you did, you would be a completely different person and you might find that your friends and relatives wouldn't want to know you any more.

The Environment

Okay. So we know that part of the reason you are shy is because genetically you are a somewhat emotional person. Why, then, does one emotional person have panic attacks and another become depressed while a third is shy? And why does one shy person fear public speaking while another fears writing? The answers to these questions are most likely found in our environment. In other words, when a person is born with a certain amount of emotionality, what form that emotionality takes will depend on that person's life circumstances.

While there are probably many things in our lives that shape the degree and form of our shyness, there are two that might be especially important: family patterns and specific experiences.

Family Patterns

When we conduct research in which we ask shy people and non-shy people about their parents, we find one particular difference. Shy adults report that their parents were more controlling and protective of them than do non-shy people. These reports have been supported by studies that have directly observed the parents of shy and non-shy children. Parents of shy children do tend to be more controlling than parents of non-shy children.

Before you go running to your parents and telling them off for making you shy, it is important to point out that this is not necessarily a one-way street. In other words, we cannot say that because your parents were over-controlling, this made you shy. Research studies suggest that the most likely pattern is a complex and circular one. That is, a loving parent will most likely respond to an emotional, anxious child by trying to help in whatever way he or she can. Remember also that emotionality is partly genetic, so it is very likely that the parent or parents are also somewhat anxious. It is hardly surprising that their help will involve trying to take over—in other words, overprotecting the child. In turn, this will give the child the message that he is not competent to handle things himself. As a result, the child will become more dependent, thus increasing the amount of help he asks for, and therefore the amount of help the parent gives.

I want to point out here that the reason for discussing all this is to help you to understand where your shyness might have come from. Assuming that you are now an adult, the way you interact with your parents has long since changed. Therefore, there is no point in having big confrontation sessions with your parents or even in assigning any blame. If this theory is correct (and there is still so much we don't know about social anxiety), then your parents and you interacted in a certain way for a variety of reasons. It is certainly no one's fault. Most important, it is now in the past and makes no difference to the treatment program we will be going through.

15

Specific Experiences

In addition to the broad messages you may have gotten from your interaction with your parents, there may also have been some more specific experiences you went through that taught you to act in a shy way.

First, we find that many of our shy clients also have somewhat shy parents. If this is so, then it may be that they are learning a lot about shyness by watching and copying their parents during the formative years. As an example, let me tell you about a client I recently saw. She was an 8-year-old girl who, as part of her problem, was very worried about making any mistakes. As a result, she tried very hard to make absolutely certain that she always did the right thing. This often stopped her from enjoying life or even getting things done. When she came in for the first treatment session following her assessment she arrived with her parents twenty-five minutes early. I asked why the family had come so early and the mother said, "We wanted to make absolutely certain that Anna wasn't late."

Many shy people have specific life experiences which can direct their later behavior.

Just think of our friend Adam who spilled a cup of coffee all over his boss. From that time on, he was terrified whenever he had to drink in front of others. Similarly, many shy people can remember disastrous dates, plays, speeches, and so on that for many years caused them to be frightened of facing a similar situation again.

SOCIAL ANXIETY, HERE AND NOW

The sections above describe some of the factors that scientists currently believe may have caused you to feel the way you do. But what is far more important is the here and now. What keeps your shyness going? To answer this question, we have to look at how shy people think, act, and feel, and how this behavior differs from that of people who are not shy. Understanding your shyness as it currently exists will help you to understand the changes you need to make to overcome it.

Socially anxious people become anxious or embarrassed in what we technically call *social/evaluative situations*. In other words, they worry about situations in which they might possibly be observed or evaluated by other people. The most common situations that frighten socially anxious people are public speaking, speaking to people in authority, dates, meeting new people, being assertive, or just "looking different." In addition, as we discussed earlier, some people are also afraid of performing specific actions in front of others such as eating or drinking in public, writing in public, or using public bathrooms.

When shy people find themselves doing or even thinking about doing something they are afraid of, such as meeting a new person, they respond in three different ways: mentally, physically, and behaviorally. Each of these responses has an important role to play in keeping the problem going, so we will discuss each in turn.

The Mental System

In a social situation, shy people differ from non-shy people mainly in the way they think about the situation.

First, shy people assume that other people will think badly of them. I will discuss this more in the next lesson. Here, I will just point out that when they are in a social situation, shy people assume that others expect them to perform perfectly and if they don't, they will see the shy people as stupid or incompetent, and will never again want to know them. In other words, shy people tend to be quite unrealistic in their thoughts about other people in social situations. Therefore, the first and most important lesson will be to teach you to think more realistically about what others are thinking of you.

Second, shy people pay a lot of attention to possible signs from others indicating that they are doing badly. In other words, in a social situation, shy people will scan other people's faces to see if there are any negative signs such as yawns or frowns. Because we only have so much attention to go around, shy people will have less to pay to what they are doing or to positive signs. Therefore, they will be better than anyone else at seeing when they doing badly, but will be very bad at seeing when they are doing well. Another component of treatment, then, will be to teach you to strengthen your attention and help you to practice focusing it on the task at hand, where it is needed, and away from non-task areas, such as what other people are doing, how you look, and so on.

Finally, shy people have a very negative view of the way they are coming across to others. When we ask socially anxious people to tell us how good they are at doing certain things, such as giving a speech, or meeting someone for the first time, they usually say they are terrible. But it may surprise you to know that other people rate the performance of shy people as just as good as anyone else's performance. In other words, shy people *assume* that others think they are bad at doing things, even though it is not true. Some of the clients I have seen have been absolutely amazed at how well they are coming across when they get some objective feedback. So, another important part of the treatment program will involve getting you some objective feedback on how you appear to others in social situations in order to prove to you that you don't look so bad.

The Physical System

When people become anxious their bodies usually respond in a number of characteristic ways. These include sweating, heart pounding, shaking, breathing fast, or feeling confused. Because shyness is a type of anxiety, these same feelings occur when the shy person faces (or thinks about) a social situation. Because the important thing for a shy person is how he is coming across to others, he will focus especially on the visible symptoms such as shaking, sweating, or blushing. There is not much we can do to stop these syptoms directly, but they will stop as you become less anxious. In addition, when you get objective feedback, you will be amazed to find that these symptoms are not nearly as noticeable as you think they are. However, the most important lesson will be to learn that having these symptoms is not nearly as awful as it feels. In other words, blushing or sweating does not mean that people will think you look silly, weak, or bad.

The Behavioral System

Finally, when shy people confront social situations, they will behave in certain ways. The most common and obvious is what we call avoidance and escape behavior. Shy people will often try to avoid social situations altogether or will get away as quickly as they can. For example, you may find yourself turning down invitations, giving in to unpleasant requests to avoid conflict, or not talking to that attractive man or woman you've been admiring for some time. Avoidance can also be more subtle, such as pretending you don't see an acquaintance as you walk down the street or not wearing a brightly colored shirt which looks just a little outlandish.

In addition, in social situations, shy people will often act less socially competent than they are able. I know I said earlier that shy people perform better than they think they do, and that is true. However, sometimes you may find that your behavior is not as outgoing as it could be. This is not because you don't know how to behave. Rather, it is a type of avoidance behavior where you don't do certain things because of your anxiety. For example, you may speak very quietly because you don't want to appear overbearing, or you may not smile at someone because you don't want to encourage her to come and talk to you. Once again, the objective feedback part of the program will help to tell you if you could do better in social situations by changing some of your behaviors. In addition, as you become more confident, you will begin to practice doing some of those things that you may have been avoiding for years.

THE PROGRAM

You should be able to see by now how important it is to have a good understanding of your own thoughts, feelings, and behaviors. I assume that at this stage you have been keeping records of these for some time. As you can see from the previous section, the coming program will involve several vital components. First, I will discuss a method of learning to think more realistically. This is possibly the most important part of the program and is probably the hardest to achieve. Therefore, you will really need to spend some time working on this component. Next, we will discuss methods by which you can practice learning to focus your attention away from the negatives and more onto the task at hand. Third, we will stop your avoidance behaviors and begin gently to confront the situations you fear. And finally, we will discuss ways in which you can obtain some clear feedback about the way you come across to others. The various components of the treatment program are listed in Table 2–1 below.

Table 2–1. Components of the Treatment Program	
Features of Social Anxiety	**Treatment Technique**
Excessive thoughts about negative evaluation	Education and training in realistic thinking
Focusing of attention onto negatives and away from the task at hand	Training in attention strengthening and increasing awareness of correct focus
Avoidance of social situations and subtle avoidance of involvement in social events	Gradual reality testing to feared situations and feedback and practicing of social skills

SUMMARY

In this lesson I provided a description of what we know about shyness and social phobia. We discussed some of the facts and figures about this problem and the possible causes. While scientists are still trying to understand exactly what makes one person more shy than others, there are several likely candidates.

- Genetically, shy people are likely to be more sensitive or emotional than the average person.

- Parents of shy children are more likely to overprotect them and not allow them to learn for themselves by making their own mistakes.

- Shy children also learn shy ways of acting by watching their parents, who themselves are often shy.

- Shy people often go through negative social experiences.

We also discussed the fact that what is more important is the ways you act now and how you differ from people who are not shy. There are three main areas.

- You probably interpret and think about situations and other people differently than do people who are not shy.

- You react more physically than do non-shy people.

- You probably avoid social situations, both obviously and subtly.

Finally, we talked about the aims of this program and the ways in which you will be learning to overcome your shyness.

21

TASKS AND CHECKLIST

✓ You should read over the previous chapter several times so that you understand the concepts clearly and have a good grasp on where your shyness comes from. Think about how the issues relate specifically to your own case, and perhaps discuss with someone or write out on a piece of paper how your personal shyness is currently being maintained.

✓ Keep completing your Social Situations Record.

THINKING
REALISTICALLY—I

I will begin this lesson with an example. Try to imagine yourself at the wedding of a close friend. This friend has asked you to say a few meaningful words during the speeches. You manage to quiet your nerves long enough to get up in front of everyone and begin talking. Try to really imagine yourself there—the sights, sounds, and smells, who might be there, what it would feel like. Just as you are getting close to the end, in a serious section, a number of people in the audience giggle. Now imagine how you would *feel* at that point. Don't try to explain it. Just think about your actual feeling. Would you feel embarrassed? Would you feel angry? How strong would your emotion be?

Now imagine that you have sat down and the person next to you leans over and whispers, "I suppose you didn't notice the waiter behind you trip and almost drop the entire tray." What would your feeling be now? I doubt that you would still be feeling embarrassed or angry.

This could have happened to any of us. But it illustrates the basic point of realistic thinking. In terms of what actually happened, *nothing changed*. In other words, you gave a speech, a waiter tripped, and some people laughed. These were the facts. But what did change was the information you had—in other words, what was going on in your head. At first, you were probably assuming that the people were laughing at you and you were feeling embarrassed or angry or both. Later, you realized that the people were probably laughing at the waiter, and you realized that there was no need to feel embarrassed. Again, though, I must point out that the actual events did not change. Only what was going on in your head changed.

This, then, is the basic rule of realistic thinking: *Our feelings and emotions are not directly caused by the things going on outside us. Our feelings and emotions are directly caused by our thoughts, attitudes, and beliefs—in other words, by what goes on inside our heads.*

The things that go on outside us may increase the likelihood of certain feelings, but only because they increase the likelihood of certain beliefs. For example, if someone pointed a gun at us, it would be very hard not to believe that we were going to be killed. Therefore, it would be hard not to be scared. But the fear is still directly caused by the belief. If we did not think that we would be killed, if we believed the gun was fake, then we wouldn't be scared.

This leads to the next point which is that *if we can learn to control our beliefs, attitudes, and thoughts, then we can learn to control our feelings.* This is what Lesson 3 is all about.

SOME POINTS TO REMEMBER

Now that you have learned the basic lesson (that our feelings are directly caused by our beliefs), there are three other points to discuss.

Extreme Thoughts Lead to Extreme Emotions

As mentioned before, emotions are directly triggered by beliefs and extreme emotions are triggered by extreme beliefs. In most cases, you won't be able to totally change your beliefs and hence totally change your emotions. However, you will learn to reduce the strength of your beliefs in order to make your emotions more manageable.

Many Thoughts Are Automatic

Most of the thoughts and attitudes that lead to your emotions will not be conscious. We describe them as *automatic*. This means that they happen extremely fast and you may not be aware of them. Because of this, it may *seem* as though you are just reacting, without any thought. But believe me, your beliefs and attitudes are playing a role. It just might take a little work for you to become aware of them.

Realistic Thinking Is Not Positive Thinking

Many people believe that realistic thinking is just like positive thinking, but this is not true. With positive thinking, everything is always described as wonderful and rosy. As a result, it doesn't work for most people because they know that life is just not like that! Realistic thinking allows for the possibility that life sometimes throws negative things our way. People do sometimes try to take advantage of us, or someone might well be laughing at us. The point is that most of the time things are not as bad as they may seem, but sometimes, when they are, then it is quite okay and very realistic to feel bad.

Importantly, when you try to change your beliefs, it will only work *if you believe it*. Therefore, positive thinking tends not to work because we usually don't believe that life is always wonderful. With realistic thinking, the idea is to weigh all the evidence and come to a logical decision about what is true. If things are truly bad, then it is quite okay to feel angry, sad, or anxious. But if things are not as bad as they seemed at first, then your feelings should also become less extreme.

HOW DO SHY PEOPLE THINK?

Shy people usually hold unrealistic beliefs in two broad ways. First, they tend to overestimate the likelihood that bad things will happen in social/evaluative situations. For example, a shy person may think that he will definitely forget all his lines if he acts in a play, or that he will make absolutely no sense when he gives a speech, or that he will be extremely boring when he goes to a dinner party. In most cases, these beliefs are not true. A shy person may forget a few lines in a play, but not all of them, or he may stumble over a few words during a speech, but generally make sense. In other words, the shy person is overestimating how likely it is that something bad will happen.

Second, shy people tend to overestimate the consequences of negative events in social/evaluative situations. In fact, this may be even more of an issue than overestimating likelihoods. For example, a shy person may believe that if he forgets some lines in a play, the audience will think that he is the worst actor ever. Or he may think that if he is boring at a dinner party, everyone will hate him. In fact, social gaffes are a common part of life. We all make them, and it is usually not a very big deal. But for the shy person, it is the worst thing in the world.

Can you think of occasions in your own life where you expected something to be far worse than it was? You can see that if you are expecting something negative to happen in a social situation and if it does, it will be an absolute tragedy, then you will be very likely to be afraid of that situation. What you need to do is to learn to think more realistically about probabilities and consequences. In this way your shyness in situations can be reduced. This lesson will be aimed at the first of these overestimates: exaggerated probabilities.

IDENTIFYING THOUGHTS

Before you can begin to change your estimates of the probability of negative events, you need to learn to identify the thoughts you are having in a situation. In some cases, this will be very obvious, but in others it may not be apparent at all.

Quite simply, whenever you notice yourself feeling shy or anxious in a social situation, you need to ask yourself, "What am I afraid of?"

or "What do I think is going to happen?" Remember in your answer that outside events do not directly cause feelings, so you need to identify your *interpretation* or *belief* about the event. So, for example, if you were going to a party and you felt anxious, you might ask, "Why am I anxious?" To then answer, "Because I am going to a party" is not enough because a party by itself does not lead to anxiety. Rather, you then need to go on and ask yourself what you are *expecting* about the party to make you anxious. You might come up with thoughts such as "I won't know anyone," or "No one will want to talk to me." These are thoughts that might make you anxious. However, they are also thoughts you can work on and try to change.

There are three other rules with respect to identifying unrealistic thoughts.

1. Try not to focus on thoughts that include feelings such as "I will feel bad." After all, feelings are what we are trying to change. Therefore, whether or not you feel bad will depend on how successful you are with your realistic thinking.

2. Also try to phrase your thoughts or attitudes in the form of what you *expect* will happen. For example, "What do I expect will happen at the party?" An answer such as, "No one will want to talk to me" can then be tested. You can, for example, think about your last party and recall whether anyone spoke to you that time. When you can clearly test a thought like this, it is quite easy to be realistic. In contrast, some people put their thoughts in the form of questions, such as "I wonder if anyone will speak with me." This makes it very difficult to apply realistic thinking because there is no way of really checking out a question like that—it's too vague. After all, it is the expectancy that something bad *will* happen that makes you anxious, not a question about *whether* it will.

3. You will need to be totally honest with yourself about your thoughts. Sometimes the thoughts or beliefs we have about a situation are so unrealistic that they sound quite ridiculous when we say them out loud. If you find this happening to you, that's good. It

means that you recognize how unrealistic your thought is and you will more easily be able to change it. Don't deny it—it is precisely because our thoughts are often unstated and automatic that they can sometimes sound quite silly.

Two Examples of Identifying Unrealistic Expectations

Let us follow the examples of our friends from the introductory chapter, Adam and Heather.

Adam was asked to a bar for a few drinks with his friends and feels quite anxious. When the therapist asked him why he was anxious, he replied "Because I don't like bars." The therapist then pointed out that for two reasons this was probably not the real thought that was making him anxious. First, a bar is an outside object that cannot directly make anyone feel a particular way. Instead, it is the interpretation of what a bar means to a person (what they expect will happen there) that causes a certain feeling. Second, that thought involves a feeling ("don't like") and this will depend on how successful the realistic thinking is. So the therapist asked Adam, "What is it about having drinks with your friends that is so frightening?" to which Adam was able to reply, "I just know that I'm going to shake when I pick up my drink." This was now a clear statement of the negative event that Adam was expecting in the situation. It is probably unrealistic because it implies that Adam will definitely (100 percent) shake, and it is something that Adam can now check out and, in this way, become more realistic about.

Heather was having some trouble paying the rent and wanted to ask her landlord for an extra week, but was afraid to approach him. When the therapist asked her why she worried about approaching the landlord, she replied, "Because he will think that I'm trying to get out of paying." This, again, is a good example of a simple and straightforward expectation that Heather will be able to work on.

ESTIMATING PROBABILITY

Once you have identified your main thought, the next step is to try to work out how likely it is that it will actually happen. In most cases, people who are socially anxious assume a 100 percent probability to their negative expectations. For example, "I will shake when I pick up my drink" implies 100%—that is, "I will *definitely* shake when I pick up my drink." In fact, things are rarely definite, so this is actually an overestimate. Obviously the higher the probability that you expect, the higher your anxiety. In contrast, the more you can convince yourself that the probability is low, the less anxiety you will experience. The key here is *belief*. Simply saying that there is a low probability is not enough. To lower your anxiety, you must believe it!

In order to come up with a correct probability and to really convince yourself of its truth, you need to look for *evidence*. In other words, once you ask yourself how likely it is that what you expect will actually happen, you need to ask yourself how you know that it's true. What evidence is there for believing your estimate of probability?

Looking at Evidence

There are many ways of looking for evidence and you need to be clever in trying to think of them all. Each situation and each expectation is unique and may have unique types of evidence. However, there are four common types of evidence that are particularly useful.

Past Experience

Obviously your best source of evidence is to think back on previous experiences you have had in the situation. For example, if you are worried that no one will talk to you at a party, you might try to think about all the previous parties you have been to and ask yourself at how many of those did *no one* speak to you. This is where realistic thinking comes in because you may find that there was in fact a time when something bad did occur. For instance, you may have actually been to a party where no one did speak with you. But if you are looking at *all* the evidence, you need to weigh that one time against all the other times when nothing went wrong. Thus, using realistic thinking, you would agree that, yes, there is a possibility that something will go wrong, but the likelihood of this is not high.

General Rules and Experience

You may also want to rely on your general experience of the way things usually are. For example, if you are worried that people will laugh at a loud tie that you are wearing, think about whether you have heard people laugh about ties before. For that matter, when was the last time you heard anyone mention a tie? Do you really think they will notice?

Alternate Explanations

Your expectation is certainly one possibility. But in any situation there are always several possibilities. Always make sure you think about all of the possible explanations in a situation and realize that yours is just one of several. For example, if you don't get a Christmas card from an old friend, one possibility is that she doesn't like you any more. However, there may be a number of other possibilities. She may have forgotten due to pressing issues, the card may have been lost, or she may have decided that she no longer wants to send cards.

Role Reversal: Putting Yourself in Someone Else's Position

This is one of the best methods of changing your probability estimates in the right circumstances. It is especially useful at times when you are worried about other people's opinions. Usually in such cases there is very little other evidence that you can use. What you need to do is to reverse roles, pretend that what happened

to you actually happened to the other person, and then work out how you would think about him or her. For example, imagine that you had forgotten an acquaintance's name when you were introducing him to someone. Your expectation might be, "He will think I am totally uninterested in him." You then need to ask yourself "How likely is this?" and one way to look for evidence would be to pretend that the situation was reversed and in fact he had forgotten your name. What would you think? Would you forgive him? The chances are that you would just assume that he had a mental lapse or you would not think about it at all. If this is so for you, why should the other person be different? One of the interesting things about shy people is that they are very forgiving of others but assume that others are not forgiving of them!

Some shy people are also not very forgiving of themselves. They may set extremely high standards for themselves and may believe that mistakes that are perfectly acceptable in others are not OK in themselves. This is particularly so for those shy people who also suffer depression. For example, you may think, "I don't mind if so and so forgets my name, but if I forget his, that's terrible." This is not a logical or realistic way to think. After all, why should you have to live by standards that are higher than everyone else's? If you automatically tend to think this way, it is important to regularly identify your underlying thoughts and also to discuss your standards for various situations with your therapist or trusted other person to try and get some perspective on them.

This is also a good place to point out that most people do not carefully and critically examine everything that people around them do. Just think about yourself—when you are mixing with people, or even when you are introduced to someone, how much of what they said, did, and looked like do you really remember one hour, one day, or one week later? If this is so for you, then why should it be any different for the people you meet? In other words, most people you interact with are probably not really taking a great deal of interest in you. This means if you make a mistake other people will very possibly not even notice and, if they do, they will probably forget about it very soon.

Two Examples of Examining Probabilities

Let us continue to look at the examples of Adam and Heather.

If you remember, Adam had realized that his expectation about going to a bar with some friends was that he would shake when he picked up his drink. Here is his conversation with his therapist:

Therapist: So how likely do you think it is that you will shake when you pick up your glass?

Adam: I know I will. I always shake when I drink with others.

Therapist: "Always" is a very extreme word. Why don't you try to remember the last ten times you went to a bar.

Adam: Well, I definitely remember shaking last time ... and the time before that. ... But now that I think about it, there was a good period a few months ago when I went out a few times and didn't shake, but I figured that was just luck.

Therapist: So, if you are being totally objective about all this, it sounds like there have been a few times when you did shake, but also several times when you did not. What probability would that give you?

Adam: When I force myself to look at it, I guess there's a moderate probability that I'll shake.

Therapist: That's certainly better than 100 percent.

Now let's look at part of Heather's session with her therapist. If you recall, Heather was worried about asking her landlord for an extra week to pay the rent and thought that he would think she was trying to get out of it.

Therapist: How long have you been renting where you are?

Heather: Oh, probably eight years or so.

Therapist: And have you ever been late with the rent before?

Heather: No, never.

Therapist: Do you have a good relationship generally with your landlord?

Heather: Yes, we usually have a pleasant chat when he comes over to fix things and he brought me some corn he had grown once.

Therapist: So, based on your knowledge of people and the type of person your landlord is, do you think it's very likely that he will think you're trying to get out of the rent?

Heather: No, I guess that's not very likely.

Therapist: Okay, let's look at other evidence. Let's pretend that the roles were reversed and that your landlord owed you money, that he didn't have a job, and that he wanted an extra week to pay. Would you suspect anything bad?

Heather: Of course not. I would feel so bad for him—I would let him take as long as he needed.

Therapist: And you say that your landlord is not a nasty person.

Heather: Not at all.

Therapist: So then why would he be likely to think badly of you?

Heather: I guess there's no reason when you put it that way.

REALISTIC THINKING RECORD

Learning to think realistically is one of the most important parts of controlling your shyness. It is also probably the hardest. Perhaps more than for any other technique, this one requires practice, practice, practice!

On p. 34 you will find a form (Table 3–1) that you can use to practice realistic thinking. Read the instructions carefully.

Event: In the first column you need to write down the situation or the event that is making you feel shy or anxious. It is very important that this column contain only the outside event as it actually occurs or is going to occur, that is, without any interpretation from you. So, for example, "being introduced to a stranger" is fine while

Table 3–1. Realistic Thinking Record—1

Event	Expectation (Initial prediction)	Evidence (How do I know)	Probability (Realistic)	Degree of Emotion (0–8)

Degree of Emotion

0	1	2	3	4	5	6	7	8
none		slight		moderate		quite a bit		extreme

34

"being embarrassed in front of a stranger" is not because it contains an emotion which of course you hope to change.

Expectation: In the next column record your first thought, attitude, or belief about the situation. This is the negative outcome that you expect or predict will happen and is the direct reason for your feeling of anxiety or embarrassment. Remember the rules we discussed earlier: (1) try not to include feelings, (2) make it a statement, (3) be honest with yourself.

Evidence: Next you need to list all of the evidence you can think of when weighing the probability for what you expect will happen. Remember the four main types of evidence (past experience, general rules, alternate explanations, role reversal) and remember to be clever in thinking up other types.

Realistic Probability: When you have looked at all of the evidence, you need to write down how likely you think it really is that your expectation will happen. Remember, this probability should be based on all the evidence you have thought of, but should also be an honest estimate. Some people might like to use actual numbers, such as 75 percent probability, 5 percent probability. However, it is okay simply to describe it in words like low probability, minimal probability, moderate probability, and so on. Use whatever makes the most sense to you.

Emotion: Finally, you need to write down the strength of your emotion after you have thought through your evidence and realistic probability. Use the same scale that you have been using in the Social Situations Record, where 0 is no anxiety or shyness at all, and 8 is the worst feeling of fear or embarrassment you could imagine. If you have been realistic and detailed in your evidence, your emotion should now be just a little lower than it was at the beginning.

To practice realistic thinking use the sheet as much as possible. Make copies for yourself and don't be afraid to use many pages. The more you practice, the easier it becomes. Try to record every example of your shyness for one or two weeks before moving on to the next lesson. Whenever possible, carry the sheet with you and record your anxiety as soon as possible after you notice it. However, if you forget to do this, or don't get an opportunity, make the recording anyway, even quite some time later. Every example will help you to learn the procedure and will help those automatic thoughts to change.

A sample form filled out by Heather is included in Table 3–2.

Some people find it difficult to remember the main types of evidence to look for, especially when they are feeling anxious (which is when they need it most). Therefore, I have listed the four types of evidence below. Copy this onto a small sheet of paper or card and carry it with you all the time. Then, if you forget the types of evidence to look for, you can look at the card.

Four Main Types of Evidence

- Past experience:
    How much has this happened before?
- General rules:
    Is this something that generally happens?
- Alternate explanations:
    What other explanations are there?
- Role reversal:
    How would you feel if this was the other way around?

Table 3–2. Heather's sample Realistic Thinking Record—1

Event	Expectation (Initial prediction)	Evidence (How do I know)	Probability (Realistic)	Degree of Emotion (0–8)
Wanting to ask landlord for extra week to pay rent	He will think I'm trying to get out of paying	I have never been late with the rent before. We get on well together and he trusts me. If the roles were reversed, I would be happy to give him an extra week and wouldn't suspect anything.	Very Low	2

Degree of nervousness or shyness

0	1	2	3	4	5	6	7	8
none		slight		moderate		quite a bit		extreme

SUMMARY

In this lesson we discussed the first steps toward learning to think more realistically.

- The main thing to remember in realistic thinking is that your feelings are directly caused by your attitude, belief, or thought about a situation, not by the situation itself.

- Extreme thoughts or beliefs lead to extreme emotions. Toning down those thoughts or beliefs will lead to less extreme emotions.

- Shy people tend to overestimate the likelihood that bad things will happen in social situations.

- To learn to think more realistically in a situation, you first need to identify your expectation.

- Next, you need to identify the evidence for that expectation. There are four main types: past experience, general rules and experience, alternate explanations, and role reversal.

38

TASKS AND CHECKLIST

✓ You need to practice realistic thinking by using the Realistic Thinking Record as often as you can. You should practice for at least a week before moving on to the next lesson. However, if you are having any difficulty or don't get many opportunities to practice, read back over this lesson and keep practicing longer before moving on to Lesson 4.

✗ You can stop the Social Situations Record if you wish, although you might find it valuable to keep it going.

LESSON 4

THINKING
REALISTICALLY—II

By now, you should be starting to feel comfortable with the idea of identifying your negative expectations and evaluating the evidence for them. One of the important aspects of this program is that if there is any lesson that you do not think you have learned properly or practiced fully, you should never feel concerned about going over it again and practicing for a while longer. Everyone moves at a different pace and there are no prizes for being the first one finished. The only prize is being able to control your shyness, which will only come by fully mastering this program. If you are working the program with a therapist, he or she will know if it is time to move on or whether you should practice for another week or so.

If you recall, shy people tend to make two major types of errors in their thinking: overestimating the probability of negative outcomes and overestimating the cost or consequence of negative outcomes. Assuming you are now getting better at realistically estimating probabilities, it is time to tackle the next type of error: consequences.

SO WHAT?

So what? Isn't that a question you have heard so many times? Most of the time, it is not meant or taken very seriously. But imagine if you honestly tried to answer that question. For example, imagine that you called someone by the wrong name and you feel mortified. But what if a friend came up at that moment and said, "So you used the wrong name, so what?" Rather than ignoring the question as we often do, imagine really trying to think about the answer. The answer to this question is the *consequence* of the negative outcome of calling someone by the wrong name. People who are not shy will probably answer something like, "I guess they'll just forget about it." On the other hand, shy people would probably think of an answer like, "They'll think I'm terribly rude."

So the way to begin to identify your assumed consequences is to follow your expectation with the question "So what?" Another good question is, "What would happen if . . . ?" For example, "What would happen if I did call someone by the wrong name?"

Let's put this together. Imagine you want to ask a person to go and have a drink with you after work and you feel nervous. Remember, the first step is to identify the expectation that is directly causing your nervousness. This might be something like, "She won't want to go." As usual, you should look at all the evidence for this belief and decide how likely it really is. You might look at the fact that she has always been pleasant to you before, that if someone asked you for a drink after work, you would go, but that you don't really know this person very well and you have never been out with her before. So, weighing all the evidence, you might decide that there is a slight to moderate chance she won't want to go. The next step is to ask yourself, "What would really happen if she didn't want to go?" You might then come up with the answer, "That would mean she doesn't like me." Do you recognize this answer? That's right—it's another expectation and you know exactly what to do with those! Obviously, you are not finished. You need to keep going and now look at the evidence that *if* she doesn't want to go for a drink with you, it means that she doesn't like you. You might look at alternative explanations. For example, might she have said no because she is busy or tired? Or you might put yourself in the other person's place. If you had turned someone down, would it necessarily be because you don't like her? Or could it be because you're shy? So, you see, the consequence of your original thought is also probably quite unrealistic. Once you realize that there is only a slight to moderate chance that she will turn you down and, even if she does, there is very little chance that it's because she doesn't like you, you should no longer feel very anxious about asking.

EXAMPLES FROM ADAM AND HEATHER

Now let's continue the examples from Adam and Heather from the previous lesson.

Adam

If you remember, Adam was thinking of going to a bar with some friends and was worried that he would shake. After discussing it briefly with his therapist, he realized that he was overestimating the chance that he would shake and that there was actually only a moderate chance that he would do so.

Therapist: So the chance that you will shake is not nearly as much as you thought. But, being realistic, we have to acknowledge that this means you might still shake. Try to ask yourself, "What would really happen if I do shake in front of my friends?"

Adam: You don't know those guys. They would think I was crazy!

Therapist: That sounds like another serious expectation to me: if I shake, the guys will think I'm crazy. Let's try to look at some evidence for that. Have you ever been with them when you did shake?

Adam: Yeah, there was one time—that was terrible, I just couldn't stop shaking.

Therapist: So what did they say? Did they say you were crazy.

Adam: I can't remember them saying anything. I'm not sure they really noticed.

Therapist: So there's another bit of evidence. How closely do you think people normally watch each other? Do you watch other people so closely that you would notice some shaking?

Adam: Sometimes I do, but not always, I guess. I suppose I'm also looking out for it because of my problem.

Therapist: So, it sounds like there's a good chance they won't even notice. And they haven't said anything before. Now try putting yourself in their shoes. What would you think if one of them was shaking?

Adam: Well, I wouldn't think he was crazy, but that's because I know what it's like.

Therapist: And they don't?

Adam: Maybe they do, but I doubt any of them have my problem.

Therapist: Imagine if you didn't have this problem and you saw a friend shake a little when he reached for a drink. What might you think.

Adam: Nothing much I guess—probably that he had a late night last night. [laughs] Or maybe I'd just think he was tired.

Therapist: So you wouldn't think he was crazy?

Adam: Not if I knew him and had seen him lots of times before.

Therapist: So the chance that your friends will think you're crazy if you shake?

Adam: My friends? Nil, I guess. Other people in the bar? Maybe they would. I guess a slight chance, but who cares?!

Heather

Heather, as you recall, was worried about asking her landlord for an extra week to pay the rent and was worried that he would think she was trying to get out of it.

Therapist: Okay, Heather, so you've said that it's not really very likely that your landlord would think that you're trying to get out of paying the rent. But let's assume that slight chance did come true and he did think that. So what?

Heather: I just couldn't look him in the eye again. I'm sure he would think I'm a mean and unreliable person.

Therapist: Is that what you would think if someone had been trying to avoid paying you money he owed?

Heather: It depends on the circumstances. Usually it would depend on what else I knew about him.

Therapist: So, in other words, you wouldn't let one instance determine your entire view of someone.

Heather: Yeah, I guess not.

Therapist: And what other information would you need about someone?

Heather: Well, I would look at his past history. Has he ever not paid me back before? And I would look at how I feel about him generally. Is he a nice person, or have I always suspected him?

Therapist: Great. Those seem like good criteria. Let's apply them to your relationship with your landlord. Have you ever not paid the rent before? Do you generally get on with him?

Heather: I knew you would say that. Of course not. I've always paid the rent in the past and Joe and I get on great.

Therapist: It doesn't sound very likely to me that Joe would think you were an unreliable person, even if he did think you were trying to get out of paying the rent. What are some alternative things he might think?

Heather: Well, he knows I don't have a job at the moment and that I'm going through a tough time. I guess he would just think it was temporary.

DOING YOUR OWN EXAMPLES

I hope that now you have a good idea of how realistic thinking works. All you have to do from here is practice!

On p. 45 (Table 4–1) you will see a monitoring form for you to record your realistic thinking. Notice that this form is the same as the one you have been using until now except that one extra column has been added, a column for the *consequence*. From now on, after you have decided on the realistic probability for your expectation, you need to ask yourself what would happen if what you expected actually did occur. Record your answer (again in terms of a statement or expectation) in the last column.

But you're not through yet! Next, write the consequence again, but this time in the expectation column, under your first expectation. Then you need to go through the same process: listing all the evidence and coming up with a realistic probability for this new expectation. Do you think you're finished? Not yet! You can now ask yourself about the consequence for this new expectation. Then rewrite the answer again in the expectation column and start again. You can keep doing this over and over, either until you run out of consequences, or until your anxiety is zero. In some situations you might have two or three levels; other times you might have twenty! Don't be afraid to use lots of paper and go all the way to the logical end. This is the only way you will really get to see just how unrealistic many of your thoughts are.

Adding in this next step (consequence) will be a difficult but really important part of learning to control your shyness, so you need to practice as much as you can in order to make it feel like second nature. As before, to help you when you are actually in the situation, we have made a list (page 46) of the types of evidence you can use to challenge your probabilities and have added the "so what" question to remind you to go on and look at the assumed consequences of your expectation. It's a good idea to photocopy this list and cut it out so that you can carry it with you at all times.

A COMPLETE EXAMPLE

Confused? Don't give up. This is not an easy technique to get completely right and it takes some time and thought. But it is very use-

Table 4-1. Realistic Thinking Record-2

Event	Expectation (Initial prediction)	Evidence (How do I know)	Probability (Realistic)	Degree of Emotion (0–8)	Consequences (What if)

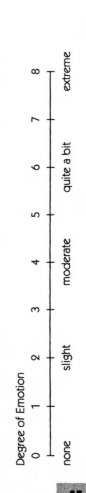

Degree of Emotion

0	1	2	3	4	5	6	7	8
none		slight		moderate		quite a bit		extreme

There is a sample monitoring form showing Jenny's recording of this example on p. 47 (see Table 4–2).

Ways to Challenge Your Beliefs

1. Examine evidence.

- *Past experience:*
    How much has this happened before?
- *General rules:*
    Is this something that generally happens?
- *Alternate explanations:*
    What other explanations are there?
- *Role reversal:*
    How would you feel if this was the other way around?

2. Then, look at consequences.

- Ask yourself, "So what if this did happen?"

46

ful once you are able to master it. Don't be embarrassed to ask your therapist lots of questions and don't be in too much of a hurry or too embarrassed to go back over the earlier sections. It might help to read through the following complete example from our friend Jenny. There is a sample monitoring form showing Jenny's recording of this example on p. 47 (see Table 4–2).

Jenny's husband, Jim, has been invited to an important business dinner with his boss and some potential clients and wants Jenny to accompany him. Jenny has been worrying about this for some time and finally sat down to examine her thoughts on the morning before the dinner.

Jenny's first expectation is that she will say something stupid. But very quickly she came up with her first piece of evidence to the contrary: that she was a high school graduate and while she is not "brilliant," she is certainly not stupid. In addition, she realized that she has been to dinner parties before, even important ones, and sure, she isn't the life of the party, but she can't remember ever really

Table 4–2. Sample Realistic Thinking Record showing Jenny's example

Event	Expectation (Initial prediction)	Evidence (How do I know)	Probability (Realistic)	Degree of Emotion (0–8)	Consequences
Dinner with Jim's work colleagues	I will say something stupid.	I have been through high school. I haven't said anything very stupid before at these things. People usually talk about every-day topics that I can handle.	Little	4	People will think Jim is stupid.
	People will think Jim is stupid.	People wouldn't make that assumption. They know how good Jim is from work.	Almost none	2	He would lose his job.
	Jim would lose his job.	Jim's boss knows he is a good worker. But someone who is stupid would probably be fired.	Moderate	2	He will never get another job.
	He will never get another job.	He is very good at his work and is well thought of. He is great at interviews.	Nil	1	

Degree of nervousness or shyness

```
 0     1     2     3     4     5     6     7     8
 |-----+-----+-----+-----+-----+-----+-----+-----|
none      slight     moderate      quite a bit      extreme
```

47

putting her foot in it. Finally, Jenny told herself that most of the time at these dinner parties, the main topics of conversation concerned fairly everyday subjects like the kids, sport, or movies, and it's pretty hard to say anything very stupid about those.

Based on these pieces of evidence, Jenny decided that there was a pretty small chance she would say anything stupid. Next, she went on to ask herself "Anyway, even if I did say something stupid, what would really happen?" Her answer, she discovered, was that she was worried that this would reflect badly on Jim and that people might think *he* was stupid. Jenny then wrote this thought down as her new expectation and looked at the evidence. "First of all, why should people connect the two of us in that way," she thought. "After all, if I thought that someone was stupid, I wouldn't necessarily assume that his partner was also stupid!" In addition, Jenny realized that these people worked with Jim and they obviously knew his talents. At this point she decided that even if people thought she was stupid, there was almost no chance they would connect that with Jim and assume that he was also stupid.

Even though Jenny was now no longer very anxious about the party, she decided she should look at her thoughts even more closely. So she asked herself what would happen if people did assume that Jim was also stupid. After quite a bit of consideration, she came up with the thought that perhaps he would lose his job. When she looked at the evidence, it was quite mixed: certainly Jim's boss knew that he was a good worker so he was not really likely to fire him. On the other hand, if Jim's boss really did believe he was stupid, he might fire him anyway. So Jenny decided that there was a moderate chance that Jim would be fired, *if* people thought he was stupid.

But the next level was the clincher. Almost before Jenny had asked herself "So what if Jim is fired?" she realized that he is very good at his work and is very well thought of in the field, so he would have no trouble getting another job.

BASIC BELIEFS

When you begin to peel away all of the levels of your beliefs by look-ing for your assumed consequences, you will often get down to a belief or sometimes a few different beliefs that just do not seem to have consequences. Usually, these beliefs are phrased more along the lines of a sort of unwritten law. For example, many people with social phobia hold the belief "everyone must like me" at the bottom of their minds. Other common beliefs include, "If I am not liked, I am worthless", or "I always have to try my hardest," and so on. We call these *basic beliefs* because most of the time, they are at the core or bottom of a series of beliefs or attitudes. Most of the time they remain completely buried and unconscious. It is only when you start to unravel them by challenging them that you might come across your basic beliefs.

You will often find that many of your situations come back to the same one or two basic beliefs. These may be ways that you have learned to live your life through experience, or they may be mes-sages drummed into you by your parents, your religion, or your cul-ture. In some cases, these basic beliefs are obviously unrealistic and as soon as you make them conscious by challenging them, you will realize how unrealistic your fears are. More often, however, these basic beliefs are hard to shake. If you come across one or two that seem to lie at the core of many of your fears, then it's very good idea to sit down and talk about them with your therapist, or if you don't have a therapist, then with a close friend or confidant. By talking through your basic beliefs with an objective outsider, you may be able to get a more realistic perspective on them. Of course, because these are beliefs, there is no right or wrong way to think, so it may well be that after discussing them, you decide that these beliefs are in fact quite acceptable and that you do not wish to get rid of them (this is especially the case if you hold strong religious or cultural values). In this case, talking about these beliefs with someone can still help you to understand more about them, and especially to see how they influence your life. I would never say that you should give up beliefs that you hold dear to your heart, but you should understand where these beliefs come from and what influence they have on your life.

Here is a sample of some common basic beliefs.

- Everyone must like me.
- I must always try my hardest.
- If I don't do really well at something, I am worthless.
- I must always be doing something useful.
- I should never have to feel bad.
- Life is worthless without a partner to share it.

SHORT CUTS

When you practice challenging your thoughts, you may often find a recurring pattern emerging. We all have our own particular issues that are important, and you may well find that your fears in social situations are controlled by the same recurring pattern of underlying thoughts. Sometimes this may be a recurring basic belief; other times, the recurring pattern emerges earlier in the challenge process. If this is the case, you may be able to develop a shortcut to your realistic thinking by jumping straight to this pattern and reminding yourself of the recurring evidence every time you notice your anxiety begin to increase. For example, after doing realistic thinking for a few weeks, Adam noticed that the same pattern of thoughts kept coming up for him and that he was tending to use the same evidence over and over. Each time he had a social engagement, he would worry that people would watch him, that he would then begin to shake, that people would then think he looked stupid (or sometimes drugged), and that ultimately, they wouldn't like him. Finally, Adam's basic belief was that he always had to be liked. After he worked through this series of thoughts many times and looked at all of the evidence, Adam became very good at realizing how unrealistic most of these

50

thoughts were. He realized that one of the most obviously unrealistic thoughts was that he would shake (he soon worked out that this was very unlikely) and that if he shook, people wouldn't like him (by reversing positions, Adam realized that even if he shook, most people wouldn't notice and even if they did, they would almost certainly think nothing much of it). So he worked out a shortcut for himself whereby each time he entered a social situation and noticed himself beginning to get nervous, he would simply remind himself of two sentences: "I know I'm not likely to shake" and "Even if I do shake, I know people aren't going to care." Because he had practiced the exercise so many times, Adam reached a point where simply saying these two sentences to himself was enough to bring down his anxiety very quickly.

In a similar way, you can also work out some shortcuts to help speed up realistic thinking once you begin to notice some patterns. However, it is very important that you practice the full technique for several weeks before you begin to use shortcuts. Shortcuts will only work if you really believe the things you say to yourself and you can only reach real belief by going through all the evidence many times.

SUMMARY

In this lesson we discussed the second part of thinking realistically: examining consequences.

- Following each expectation in a situation, you can identify the consequence of that expectation by asking yourself the question, "So what?" The answer to this question identifies another expectation that can be challenged in terms of its evidence.

- At the bottom of all of your beliefs, you may come across one or more basic beliefs. Learning to identify and look more realistically at them can be a major part of learning to think more realistically.

- Once you become very experienced at your realistic thinking, you may be able to identify some common patterns in your thinking that can be used as shortcuts to reduce your anxiety.

TASKS AND CHECKLIST

✓ Continue to practice your realistic thinking and include consequences, using the new Realistic Thinking Form. Keep using this form for at least the next two weeks.

5

TRAINING YOUR ATTENTION

Imagine the following scene: you are sitting with a group of people and telling a story about your last vacation. All of a sudden, you become aware of the fact that everyone is looking at you. You become very self-conscious, you begin to sweat and shake, your mind feels totally confused, and you begin to ramble in your story. Does this sound familiar? Scenes like this are all too common for people with social phobia. In this section we will look at why this happens and what you can do about it.

Scientists are beginning to recognize the important role that attention plays in this type of situation. Just go back for a minute to the scene. Try to imagine it again and think about where you might be focusing your attention, once you become aware of everyone's eyes on you. If you are very anxious, I'll bet you will be focusing it on two places. First, you will be imagining how you look to those around you. You will probably have a mental picture of yourself as covered in sweat, appearing wooden, and generally looking nervous. Second, you will probably be focusing right on the eyes of the group. You will be seeing those eyes as really piercing, and you will be assuming the group is thinking all sorts of negative things about you. All of this probably feels like a wild, confusing mess in your mind, a jumble of thoughts and images. But it feels like this because your mind is trying to do three things at once: (1) it is trying to concentrate on how you look and what you are doing, to make sure you don't look silly, (2) it is trying to work out what the others in the group are thinking and it is focusing really hard on making sure that no one appears bored, cynical, or in any way negative, and (3) of course it is focusing on trying to remember the next part of the story. Because there is so much going on in your mind at the same time, everything feels jumbled and confused.

When you focus on the first two areas described above—that is, on how you look and on what others are thinking—you take away most of your attention from the job you are doing: your story. It's no wonder then, that you will begin to ramble, that you might lose your thread, or that you might stammer and stutter. What you need to be doing is focusing all of your attention on your story. If you can do that, you will find that you will do a much better job of telling the story and you will feel far less self-conscious. You should not need to focus attention on the other people or on how you look. If you can focus your full attention on the job you are doing (telling your story), then the other things can take care of themselves. This is the next step in learning to overcome your shyness.

Let's look at a couple of other examples. Imagine that you are in an important meeting at work and you want to ask a question. You should be concentrating fully on what the current speaker is saying so that you can remember it later and so that you can formulate your question appropriately at the right time. Instead, it is very likely that you will be thinking hard about exactly how to best phrase your question (in other words, part of your attention will be focused on yourself) and also on how you are going to come across to the other people in the meeting ("Will I sound dumb?", "Have I missed the point?"). As a result, there is a very good chance that you *have* missed the

54

point and that your question may not make a lot of sense, because you haven't been focusing on the task at hand, that is, on what the speakers are saying.

A similar example might be found if you are playing a sport in front of an audience. In many cases, you might find that you play a lot worse than usual in this situation. Again, this is because you should be focusing all of your attention onto the crucial part of the sport, such as the ball, perhaps. Instead, you might find that your attention is divided between imagining what the audience is thinking of you and your mental picture of how you look.

ATTENTIONAL EXERCISES

You can think of your attention almost like a muscle in your body. We all know that muscles, when they are not used, become soft and flabby. In exactly the same way, your ability to concentrate and focus your attention onto particular things also becomes weak without regular use. People whose lives and jobs involve long periods of concentration, such as chess players or air traffic controllers, will be much better at focusing their attention where they want to or need to than the rest of us, just as people whose jobs involve hard physical labor will be fitter and stronger than most other people. Therefore, for many of us, before we can learn to focus our attention away from ourselves and others and onto the task at hand, we will need to strengthen our attention by engaging in attentional exercises.

Any procedure that requires concentration can be used to strengthen your attention. There is no magic here. Like all our techniques, the key is practice. The technique that I recommend is a type of simple meditation. The value of this is that in addition to helping you train your attention, you can also use this procedure to help you with general relaxation.

The first thing to do is to give yourself the right atmosphere in which to practice. Later, you can make things tougher for yourself, but to begin, you will need to make things as comfortable as possible. Take the phone off the hook, get the temperature just right, lock yourself away from other people and interruptions, and put on some comfortable clothes. Find a nice, comfortable chair (it is generally best not to do this while lying down, or you are likely to fall asleep!).

Once you are ready, you can begin. The actual meditation procedure is very simple to explain, but not necessarily so easy to do. You simply allow your breathing to relax, then you mentally count "one" when you breathe in and imagine the word "relax" when you breathe out; then "two" when you next inhale, "relax" when you exhale; "three," and so on. Try to picture the numbers and the word "relax" in your head as you go. This is where the attentional training part comes in. Ideally, you should be able to focus all of your attention on the images of the numbers and the word "relax" without any other thoughts coming into your mind.

I guarantee that when you first begin this technique you will find many other thoughts coming into your head ("When I'm done, I'll have to take out the trash", "What should I have for dinner tonight?" "I mustn't forget to call Joe" and so on). This is all right to begin with.

Whenever you notice your thoughts drifting away from the numbers, simply let those thoughts go and bring your mind back to them. It is probably best to begin with the number "1" again rather than worrying about where you were up to. In the same way, when you reach the number "10," go back to the beginning again. Otherwise, you will find that you try to compete with yourself each time to go further and further. The point of this exercise is not competition, but to reach a calm, relaxed state in which your mind is focused on nothing but the task at hand—the numbers and the word "relax." The more you practice this technique, the better you should find yourself at being able to focus your attention without other thoughts coming into your mind. As with any exercise, of course, you will have good and bad days. Sometimes, perhaps because you are stressed or tired, you will find it harder than other times to focus your attention. If this happens, the main thing is not to give up, but simply to keep practicing, knowing that you can't expect as much as usual.

Practice this meditation technique at least twice a day for at least ten minutes at a time. Of course, the more you practice, the better you will get. This is a great technique for helping you get to sleep if you have difficulty with this, but it should not be counted as one of your practices. Practices need to be at specific, set-aside times, preferably when you are not too tired and are not trying to rush off to do something else. It is a good idea to keep a record of your practices. I have included a possible form to use on p. 58 (see Table 5–1).

As you begin to get better at focusing your attention and excluding other thoughts, you should also gradually begin to increase the difficulty of your practices. This is like adding weights in weight lifting or going longer distances in swimming training. Until you start to get the hang of it, you should make conditions as easy as possible so as not to get distracted. This might last for one week or several weeks, depending on how hard you practice. Once you are feeling confident with your meditation and are able to focus for at least a few minutes without losing concentration, you can begin to add more difficult elements to your practices, one at a time. For example, you might begin to practice in a slightly less comfortable chair, and then on the floor, or even eventually standing up. Or you might practice with the door or window open, and then eventually with the television or radio on. Remember, the point is ultimately to be able to focus your attention in all sorts of difficult, real-life situations. So the more you can begin to approximate these conditions in your practices, the better you will be.

OTHER PRACTICE

What we have discussed above is the formal procedure for strengthening your attention. However, you will find your attention improving even more if you also begin to incorporate attentional focus into your daily life. This will help you get used to using attentional focus in real-life situations.

Table 5–1. Form for recording Attentional Training Practice

Date	Time	Duration	Concentratrion (0–8)	Comments

Degree of Emotion

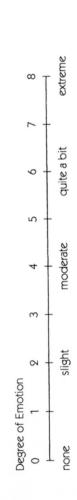

```
0    1    2    3    4    5    6    7    8
|----+----+----+----+----+----+----+----|
none    slight    moderate    quite a bit    extreme
```

One of the main techniques is to practice short bursts of your meditation exercise throughout the day whenever you can. We call these *mini-meditations* and you can do them for any amount of time, perhaps only a few seconds, whenever you get a break in your day. For example, while you are sitting at traffic lights on your way to work you can begin to do your breathing and counting for the ninety seconds or so that you are stopped. Or you could practice focusing your attention on counting your steps as you walk from office to office at work or as you walk to the front door to collect the mail. Of course you must remember that it will be much harder to focus your attention during these mini-meditations than during your usual longer practices. But, partly for this reason, this makes them a very good form of practice.

In addition to mini meditations, you might also practice doing more attention-focusing types of games and tasks in your day. For example, you might try doing some crosswords, balancing your budget, or even reading some fairly mundane material. In each case, you should try to go for longer and longer periods without your thoughts drifting off the topic.

APPLIED PRACTICE

After you have practiced your attention strengthening exercises for a while, you should start to apply your attention focus to social situations. When you find yourself in situations where you have to perform socially in some way, for example, talking to your boss, presenting a report, or meeting new people, try to focus all of your attention on the task you are performing and away from any thoughts or images about how you look or about what the other people are thinking of you. For example, suppose you go to a dinner and are introduced to two new people. Try to focus your attention on such things as what the people's names are, their interests, or on the questions they ask you. Try not to dwell on things like your own appearance, or on scanning their faces and bodies for signs of disapproval. Just as in your practices, when these negative thoughts come into your mind, don't panic. Just let them go and bring your attention back to the task at hand. Of course, doing your realistic thinking beforehand will help to make these things less important anyway, which, in turn, will make it easier for you to avoid focusing attention on them.

It is also important not to try to keep a mental check on whether you are doing your attentional focus correctly. In other words, when you are in a social situation, and you make sure that your attention is focused fully on the task at hand, try not to check mentally on how you are doing. Checking how you are doing usually involves thinking consciously about your thoughts and trying to remember whether you have thought about the "wrong thing" or not. Of course, as soon as you do this, you stop focusing on the task at hand. It is important to try to keep your mind on the task at hand and not let any other thoughts enter your mind (even thoughts about whether you are focusing properly).

Of course, as with any procedure, it is important not to expect instant results. Focusing your attention away from negative thoughts and onto the task at hand is a difficult exercise when you are in a situation that frightens you. Therefore, it will take time and practice before you will be able to do this consistently or successfully.

SUMMARY

In this lesson we discussed the role of attention in increasing your anxiety in many situations.

- When you perform a task in a social/evaluative situation, your mind will often be focused away from where it should be (the task) and on how you are coming across to the audience and also what other people are thinking of you.

- The first step to overcome this problem is to strengthen your attention so that you are better able to control where you focus it.

- You learned an attention strengthening exercise in the form of a meditation procedure.

- When you are more confident in being able to manipulate your attentional focus, you should intentionally begin to pay more attention to the task at hand when you are in social/evaluative situations.

61

TASKS AND CHECKLIST

✓ You need to practice your meditation exercise twice per day for 10 minutes at a time and record this practice for at least the next two weeks.

✓ Continue to complete your Realistic Thinking Records.

REALITY TESTING

Let's get back to realistic thinking for a moment. By now you should be getting into the habit of challenging your thoughts each time you get nervous. You should really be good at identifying the evidence for every expectation you have, looking at the consequences, and then identifying evidence for them. But is this enough? Are you really able to convince yourself that what you are afraid of probably won't happen? Many people find that no matter how practiced they are at challenging their thoughts, they just can't quite get over that last niggling doubt that something bad will happen.

This is quite normal. After all, how often do we learn life's lessons by simply thinking something? When you learned to drive, did you learn it all by going through it in your mind? I doubt it. You probably thought about the basics and discussed it with whoever taught you, and then went out and just did it. Sure, at first you would have been pretty inept, but the more you practiced, the better you became.

That's exactly how it is with shyness as well. If something makes you nervous, you first need to go through it carefully in your mind (realistic thinking) and then you need to go and try it out for yourself. We call this part *reality testing*. By doing reality testing for your fears, you are actually collecting your own evidence for your expectations. Remember, with your realistic thinking and your strengthened attention, you are going to be even better at interacting with people than you were before.

As usual, let's look at an example. Let's imagine a little girl, Amy, who is 2 years old and whose father is taking her for her first swim. Amy may have been scared and crying before she even got to the water. Then when Dad carried her down and put her feet in, she might have started screaming. At that point, Dad had a choice. He could have turned around and taken Amy out of the water and said not to cry, she didn't have to go back today. But what would that have done for her? Most likely, it would have taught her that water really is a bad and dangerous thing. The next time Dad tried to take Amy back to the water, it would have been even harder. On the other hand, when Amy began to scream, Dad could have tried to comfort her and relax her, but most important, he could have stayed there and made sure that she did not run away. What would have happened then? Well, most likely Amy would have screamed for a little while, then cried a bit and, after a while, once she realized that nothing bad was really happening to her, she would have calmed down. If Dad had done this, then the next time he wanted to take Amy swimming, she may have cried again, but it would probably not have been for as long or as much. Dad could then have taken her a little further into the water. Again, Amy might have gotten scared, but she would eventually calm down and realize that it wasn't so bad. If Dad kept doing this, then it wouldn't be long before Amy was driving everyone crazy wanting to go to the water all the time. But if Dad gave in to her cries and let her run away, it would be a long time before her parents ever got Amy back to the water.

This is exactly how it is with shyness. When you avoid doing something because you are shy or embarrassed about it, you are making it even harder for yourself the next time. This is because when you avoid doing something, your mind interprets it to mean that it must have been really terrible. So all the realistic thinking in the world is not going to help if you are avoiding things at the same time.

Like most of the techniques in this program, this one is also common sense. How often have you heard people say that if you fall off a bike, get back on, or if you have a car accident, go back and drive as soon as possible? Clearly, when you avoid things or run away from them, you very quickly blow them out of proportion in your mind and they become harder than ever to deal with. On the other hand, the more you do something, the easier it becomes. Even when something goes wrong, it is hardly ever as bad as you imagined it would be (remember the consequence part of your realistic thinking). Therefore, the next part of learning to control your shyness involves beginning to intentionally do things that make you feel self conscious, nervous, and shy. Sounds cruel doesn't it? Maybe, but it's the only way to build total confidence. There is an old saying, "There is no gain without pain" and unfortunately that is true here as well.

SOME POINTS TO REMEMBER

The basic technique in this lesson is simple. You simply need to recognize what makes you shy, nervous, or worried and then force yourself to do those things. However, there are particular ways of doing this and certain things you should keep in mind that make it both easier and more effective.

One Step at a Time

Remember our example of Amy and the water, how Dad took Amy into the water a little way at a time. Each time, Dad waited until Amy was relaxed and comfortable with that step before going a little deeper. Now Dad could have simply thrown Amy into the deepest part straight away and, as long as Amy didn't drown, she would probably have eventually gotten used to it and calmed down. However, this would have been a pretty horrible way to go and neither Dad nor Amy would have been very happy with each other.

The same principle applies to you. You could put a lampshade on your head, paint yourself blue, and walk down Main Street singing "Yankee Doodle." As long as you didn't get arrested, you would probably eventually relax and learn that it doesn't matter what people think of you. But this would be a pretty tough thing to do and I doubt that you would ever do it.

A much better way to approach reality testing is to try to think of different things that make you anxious and then begin with the one that is the least difficult to cope with. When you are comfortable with that, you can go on to the next one, and so on. By doing it in this way, you will learn not to worry about what people think of you, but you will be able to do it at *your* pace and under *your* control. This process is described in more detail a little later.

Stay in the Situation

If you go somewhere that makes you feel a little shy, such as a party, and then leave as soon as your shyness has reached its peak, it will be harder than ever to do it again. In fact, you would be making your problem worse. One of the important points to remember with reality testing is to stay in the situation until your shyness starts to decrease. So, for example, if you go to a party and you are feeling nervous, you need to force yourself to stay there until you begin to relax and get used to the situation. Then you can leave—although by then you probably won't want to!

The situation in the preceding paragraph is the "ideal." Ideally you want to try to stay in a situation until you begin to calm down. However, it is not always possible to so. For example, you might be nervous about saying hello to your neighbor. Using reality testing, this is exactly what you would then do. But saying hello doesn't take very long. So you can't possibly stay there until you calm down because the whole thing might only take a second. Obviously, you need to stay in the situation if the situation allows it. If not, just do what you can. It is still better to reality test in some way than not to do it at all.

One other point. Sometimes you will find yourself in a situation that you just did not anticipate and you will find that it is just too hard for you. If you feel that you absolutely *have to* get out of a situation, then you should do so. It is not the end of the world, and we have to be realistic about things. But if you do escape from somewhere, make sure you try to do it again as soon as possible. In addition, if possible, try not to competely escape but try to just back off a little. For example, let's assume you were going to try to say something in a meeting. When you get there, you find that the head of the whole company is there and you just can't bring yourself to say anything. That's fine—things change. But rather than excusing yourself and leaving the meeting entirely, why not at least try to stay there, even if you don't actually say anything?

Repeats

Doing something once is usually not enough to overcome your anxiety completely. Most of us need several exposures to a situation to feel totally comfortable. So another key to reality testing is to repeat your testing many times. Don't just say hello to your neighbor once; make it a part of your life. If you do something only once, it's very easy to tell yourself that you got through it by luck or because it was different that day. When you do it over and over, you have to eventually tell yourself that you are now in control.

Ups and Downs

If you repeat your reality testing for a particular situation, you will find, in general, that each time it will be easier and easier to do it. However, that pattern, steadily getting easier and easier each time, is the ideal. Unfortunately, it doesn't always work that way in reality.

We all have good and bad days. Sometimes we feel strong and confident and other times we feel insecure and unsure of ourselves. This could happen for a whole variety of reasons. Maybe you slept badly last night, or perhaps something went wrong in your life, or maybe you are just in a bad mood. The important thing is not to let the bad times take over completely. When you have a bad day (or several), you need to recognize that it is just that—a temporary bad patch. Realize that you will not be able to do the same things on those days as you can on your good days and be realistic. Remember your realistic thinking and set your goals a little lower. The important thing is to *do something*, even if it is less than you were doing before on a good day.

Be Aware of Avoidance

Everyone knows what it means to avoid something. It means not to go there at all, right? Well, only partly. In fact, there are many, many ways of avoiding and some of them can be very subtle. It is these subtle types of avoidance that are particularly important in shyness. Let's look more closely at the example of going to a party. You could avoid the party entirely by turning down the invitation and not going. But, on the other hand, you could go and still find yourself avoiding in more subtle ways when you get there. For example, you could go to the party and sit in the corner by yourself all night. This would be avoiding mixing with people even though you were actually at the party. Or you could talk only to the few people you know well. This would be avoiding meeting new people. Your avoidance could even be more subtle than these examples. For example, you might talk to people only about certain subjects that you feel comfortable with and keep quiet when the conversation turns to more difficult topics. Similarly, you might make sure you dress in entirely the "right" way and avoid wearing anything unusual.

The important point is that within a broad situation such as a party, there might be many other "sub-situations" (for example, new

68

people, unusual conversation topics, and so on) that you are also avoiding. When you do your reality testing, you will need to be aware of all the little things that you do that can be called avoidance and you will need to try to stop all of them. The key is *honesty.* Everyone has different fears and only you know what sorts of things you are avoiding. But if you keep avoiding them, only you lose out. You need to be totally honest with yourself about your avoidance and you need to test out all the different things that you avoid. Of course, as I said before, this does not all have to be done at once. Your reality testing should be organized in a gradual way. But eventually you should work your way through all of your avoidances.

YOUR STEPLADDER

As I mentioned before, you do not have to jump into the deep end straightaway when doing reality testing. It is much easier and more pleasant to go at a comfortable pace. Therefore, the first part of reality testing is to make some stepladders for your fears. There are three measures to follow.

1. The first is to sit down with a piece of paper and write down the broad types of things that make you feel shy, nervous, or embarrassed. For example, one might be giving speeches, presentations, and talks.
2. Next, try to brainstorm as many examples of these broad categories as you can. Don't be inhibited. Let your mind go free and try to think of as many things as possible. The situations or items you write down should be specific actions, behaviors, or settings, such as talking to the receptionist at work, not general or vague ones, like feeling insecure. If you are having trouble getting started, someone else who knows you really well can often help. Remember also about subtle avoidance. Don't forget to write down those little things that make you nervous, such as cutting your hair a different way, standing at the front of a crowd, or wearing a warm

sweater (because you are more likely to blush or sweat). At the same time, you don't need to be too obsessive about it. Anything you may have forgotten, you can always add later.

For each broad heading, try to come up with at least five (preferably more) specific situations that make you feel shy. It is a good idea to make sure that all different degrees of difficulty are represented. In other words, some of the items you come up with should make you feel only a little nervous, while others may make you feel terrified.

For example, for the broad category of "giving speeches, presentations, and talks," you might come up with the following six specific situations: (1) making a formal presentation at work, (2) making a speech at a public speaking club, (3) telling a joke to a small group of friends, (4) acting as a disk jockey at a friend's party, (5) reading out the budget for your local group meeting, (6) practicing a speech in front of your family. All of these situations or activities are things that might make you nervous or embarrassed and you might find yourself avoiding doing them. But notice that each one is different in terms of how frightening it is. Notice also that each one is written as a very specific situation and action.

3. The final step is to write each of the situations within a broad category in order of how frightening it is. Start with the easiest at the bottom and end with the hardest at the top. You should now have a list of connected situations going from easiest to hardest: here is your stepladder. Of course you will probably end up with several stepladders, one for each category of fears.

DOING REALITY TESTING

Once you have worked out a stepladder (or several) for yourself, it is time to begin practice. This simply means starting with the easiest situation (at the bottom of the ladder) and doing it. Let's say for the category of "giving speeches, presentations, and talks" your easiest situation was to practice a talk in front of your family. You would therefore need to ask several members of your family to get together and listen to you present a speech. Then simply present the speech to them. Make sure it is not too short and that you have time to get used to the situation. If you are feeling particularly nervous, you might try your realistic thinking before beginning.

When you decide to enter a situation or perform an action for reality testing, it is best if it makes you feel mildly to moderately anxious. Any less, and you really are not learning very much. More, and you will find yourself making excuses to back out of it. If you find that your next situation on the stepladder is very frightening, then it is obviously too big a step and you should try to think of ways to make it a little easier, as a between step.

Once you have done your first situation, say presenting a speech to your family, you need to repeat it several times. Organize your family to meet together again for another speech tomorrow night or in a few days. But make sure you don't stop. Keep doing it over and over until you get to the point where the situation no longer makes you feel very anxious. Then it is time to move on to the next step.

What I have described above is the ideal way to do reality testing. Begin with the first step and repeat it several times before moving on to the next. This is great if you can organize it. Unfortunately, life and social situations aren't always so neat. Often you may find that you just can't organize the very next item on the stepladder. For example, you may find that most of your family is busy and you can't get them together again for a week or more. On the other hand, sometimes higher items on your stepladder just happen to come up a bit too early. For example, the treasurer of your group might be sick and might call and ask you to read out the budget. When these things happen, you just have to be flexible. If you can't do one item on your stepladder at the moment, think about doing the next one, or try to think of an alternative. You can always come back to the earlier step later, or you may find that it is no longer a problem for you once you have done the higher steps. Similarly, if a harder step comes along, think about whether you feel ready to have a go at it. After all, with social situations you often need to grab the opportunity when it presents itself.

ADAM'S STEPLADDER

Do you remember Adam from our first section? Adam's main problems involved fears of eating, drinking, and writing in front of other people because he was worried that he would shake and do something that he felt was stupid (like drop his food). Adam made up different stepladders for his fears of eating in front of others, drinking in front of others, and writing in front of others. Part of Adam's stepladder for writing in front of other people is shown in the list below.

8. Filling out order forms in front of important clients
7. Filling out the pay forms in front of the work accountant
6. Opening up a new bank account
5. Signing a credit card in front of shop assistants
4. Applying for a credit card
3. Signing my name in front of the secretary at work
2. Jotting down my name and phone number in front of an acquaintance
1. Copying out a written passage in front of my wife

There are several things to observe about Adam's stepladder. First, notice how each item is clearly specified and is a practical, doable task. These tasks are organized so that the most difficult is at the top and the least difficult at the bottom. Adam's job now is to do the bottom item over and over until it no longer bothers him greatly, then move on to the next item. You can also see that some of the items may be a little difficult to organize. For example, item 2—jotting down his name and phone number for an acquaintance—is not an easy thing to manufacture. So Adam skipped this item but kept it in mind so that as soon as he saw an opportunity, he did write down these things for someone who wanted them. Finally, Adam found that some of the items could be broken down even further into sub-items. For example, regarding signing his credit card receipts in front of shop assistants, Adam realized that some shop assistants made him more anxious than others. For example, he found older, motherly women to be less threatening, whereas young, attractive women were very difficult. So, at first, he looked for shops where older, kinder-looking women worked and later he approached shops that employed young women.

JENNY'S STEPLADDER

If you remember, Jenny is a mother of three and is married to Jim. Jenny is somewhat shy and retiring, but still manages to do most things. She really just wants to build a little more self-confidence and be a little more outgoing. Jenny decided that her problems fell into three broad areas: not wanting to stand out in front of others, not being good at mixing with people, and always needing to be in control of her actions and feelings. Listed below is part of her stepladder for learning not to need to always be in control.

---

7. Drinking some alcohol at a party
6. Getting on a fast fairground ride and screaming
5. Crying at a sad movie in public
4. Getting on swings or rides with my kids
3. Greeting male friends more affectionately (kissing, hugging)
2. Greeting female friends more affectionately (kissing hugging)
1. Crying at a sad movie in private

Like Adam's list, you can see that Jenny's items are practical and doable. You can also see that Jenny has divided certain acts according to the nature of circumstances. For example, crying in public is quite a bit harder than crying in private.

GETTING STARTED

At this point you should be ready to start building stepladders and practicing reality testing. The first step, of course, is to build one or more stepladders. Remember, they do not have to be completely thorough before you start practicing. You can always add and modify later.

Once you have decided what your first few tasks will be, you need some commitment. Don't forget Lesson 1 on motivation. It's very easy to put things off, especially if they are a little difficult. You need to commit yourself to doing these tasks and, if you find yourself having trouble, you need to try to enlist the help of friends or family. It's a very good idea to plan out your practices ahead of time. For example, Adam decided to see his secretary on Tuesday and Thursday and sign forms in front of her, and he planned with his wife that at three different times the following weekend, he would write passages from a book in front of her.

Finally, you should keep a record of your reality testing practices. This is very important so that you can look back and see the changes you have made and what sorts of things worked and what didn't. I have included a sample recording form on p. 75 (see Table 6–1). Take note of exactly what you did, when you did it (including how long it took), and how nervous you both expected to be and actually were. You might also then jot down any comments about the experience. The Comments column is the ideal place to note such things as subtle forms of avoidance you may have engaged in, any coping techniques you used, any unexpected occurrences in the situation, any last-minute changes you made to your plans, and your general confidence and mood at the time.

Table 6–1. Form for recording Reality Testing

Situation/Event	Date/Time	Duration	Expected Anxiety (0–8)	Actual Anxiety (0–8)	Comments (e.g., unforeseen occurrences, subtle avoidance, coping strategies, etc.)

Expected/Actual Anxiety

0	1	2	3	4	5	6	7	8
none		slight		moderate		quite a bit		extreme

SUMMARY

In this lesson you learned about Reality Testing, a technique to help provide you with real-life experience by encouraging you to engage in those behaviors that you may be avoiding.

- First make stepladders by brainstorming many situations and actions that you currently fear or avoid and organizing them in order, from easiest to hardest.

- Then engage in Reality Testing by beginning with the first of these situations and gradually working your way up the ladder.

- In doing Reality Testing, there are several guides to keep in mind:
  1. Do it gradually, one step at a time.
  2. If possible, try to stay in a situation until you start to calm down.
  3. You will need to repeat the same step on the stepladder several times before you are through with it.
  4. Don't be discouraged by bad days.
  5. Be honest with yourself about what really makes you anxious in a situation and look out for subtle avoidance.

76

TASKS AND CHECKLIST

✓ Make as many stepladders as you need to cover all of your areas of avoidance.

✓ Begin with the first step of each stepladder and schedule times for beginning your Reality Testing. Keep records of your practice.

✓ Keep practicing and recording your attention training.

✗ You can stop recording Realistic Thinking if you feel comfortable with it. But don't forget to keep using it regularly, and go back to recording any time you feel it is no longer working.

7

GETTING FEEDBACK AND IMPROVING PERFORMANCE

Every now and then when we do something in our lives, we come away afterwards thinking something like "I really blew that one." While this is a normal part of life, shy people tend to do this more than other people, especially following social interactions. For example, people who are shy often think that they are very bad at public speaking, at hosting a party, at telling a joke, or at a whole range of other things having to do with performing in front of others. As a result, they often avoid doing these things because they "know" they will do them badly, or they do them and then come away thinking, "I did that so badly that they must think I'm a real idiot."

There are several points to make here. First, you must remember your realistic thinking practice. The relevant issue is the "so what" part. "So what if I bored people a little when I was speaking. Does that really mean they will think I'm an idiot, or will they just think I'm not very good at public speaking?" or "So what if I forgot that gentleman's name when I was introducing him. Will he even remember five minutes from now, and even if he does, will he think I'm totally stupid just because I had a mental blank?" By now you should be getting good enough at your realistic thinking to realize that doing things less than perfectly is not necessarily a tragedy. Just because you don't do something well should not mean that people will think you are a total idiot in all aspects of your life.

However, there is another very important point to make here. One of the most common findings in research into shyness and social phobia is that shy people have a tendency to *underestimate* their performance in social situations. In other words, when shy people do something in a social situation, like tell a joke, afterwards they believe that they did a much worse job than other people think they did.

Let me give you an example of one of the research studies from our clinic. We asked a group of people with clinically diagnosed social phobia and another group of people without social phobia to present a three-minute speech to an audience. The speech was about anything they wanted and they were given two minutes to prepare. The audience consisted of both people with social phobia and people without it. After each person's speech, the speaker was asked to rate herself on a number of items asking about her own performance (e.g., how good was your eye contact, did you keep the audience interested, and so on). The audience also rated each speaker on the same items. We were then able to compare the ratings that each speaker gave herself with those made by the audience for this same person. What we found was that people with social phobia rated their own performance much worse than they were rated by the audience.

What this tells us is that if you are anxious in social situations, you probably *think* you are doing worse than you really are. That is, other people do not look at your performance nearly as critically as you think they do. In fact, most people probably do not take as much notice of you as you may think. While you may feel as though everyone is watching you carefully and critically analyzing every action you take, it is probably more likely that most people in a social situation are not taking any notice of you at all or are keeping only half an eye on you.

Finally, the last point to be made here is that perhaps you are right. Maybe, in some situations, you really don't perform as well as you could. This is a case in which learning new ways of acting and practicing those new ways can really help. For example, learning how to give good public speeches, or even learning to tell a joke in the best possible way can really help to build your confidence.

FEEDBACK

So how do you find out which of the above possibilities is true? Are you really quite good at certain things but think you are not? Or is there room for you to really improve? Or perhaps both!

What you need is to get feedback about your social performance in various situations. Of course, one of the best ways for you to get feedback is to ask other people. Sometimes you might go around and ask a number of other people how they felt about your performance. Other times, you might have a special person, perhaps a husband or wife, brother or sister, you feel close enough to to ask for an honest evaluation. The person who gives you feedback must be someone you trust to be honest. It is very easy for you to disbelieve him or her, especially if the feedback is very positive. Therefore, make sure you tell your raters that you want totally honest feedback and tell them why. While you do want the feedback to be honest, it is also important to choose someone you trust to be gentle and kind. Sometimes people get so carried away looking for problems with your performance that they come up with a long list of picky little negatives. It is much better to tell your rater that you want a balanced view of how you performed. You want to know both the negatives and the positives. Be honest if there were problems, but don't go looking for them exclusively. It is also a good idea to ask your rater to give you feedback about your real, underlying fears, such as "Did I look like a total idiot?" or "Did I sound totally incoherent?" Remember, very few people are perfect at, let's say, engaging people in conversation, but that does not mean that others will think they are stupid or incompetent.

Asking someone for feedback about your performance will take a lot of courage. None of us likes to hear criticism and very few people like to draw attention to themselves and encourage evaluation. But getting honest and accurate feedback is essential to helping you manage your shyness. As we have been discussing, you will very possibly find that the feedback is not nearly as negative as you expect. But you also need to mentally prepare yourself for the possibility of negative feedback. Listen carefully to the feedback and use your realistic thinking. Remember, just because someone finds some faults in your performance does not mean that you and your performance are completely hopeless. Rather than dwelling on any negatives in the feedback, try to see it as an opportunity to improve the way you come across to others.

One of the most useful aspects of getting good feedback is to sit down with your rater beforehand and discuss the sorts of things which she should be looking for. Discuss together what types of things might make someone good at what you are about to do and make a list of good and bad behaviors for your rater to judge. For example, if you were going to try to tell a joke later that evening, you might plan for your rater to think about such things as how loud and clear your voice was, how well you held people's gaze and attention, how patiently you built the joke, and how clearly you delivered the punch line. She might then also rate whether you made a complete fool of yourself. Hopefully, the "scores" will be quite good and then this will tell you that you are better at telling jokes than you thought you were. But if you don't rate very well, you will then be able to discuss with your rater exactly where you could improve and what sorts of things you should work on. We will discuss this in more detail later.

As usual, what I have been talking about in the previous paragraphs is the "ideal." Finding a special person whom you trust and who is willing and able to go with you to social events and rate your performance is fantastic if you can find one. But some of us will not be able to find a person like this and even if we can, this person will hardly be able to go with us to all of our social events. So what do we do in those less-than-ideal situations? Basically, the answer is improvise. The same principles apply. You need to get feedback about your performance and you want it to be honest, caring, and very specific. There are often ways in various situations where you can get approximations of this ideal. For example, if you give a business presentation, you can ask your boss for feedback. Most bosses would be thrilled if an employee came to them saying, "I would like to work on my presentation skills because I want to keep improving. Can you sit down with me for a few minutes and give me your thoughts on my strengths and weaknesses?" With a statement like that I can't imagine that any boss will think badly of you. In fact, you would probably score points. Alternately, you could ask a friend who happens to be there to provide feedback or to scout around and find out how other people saw you. Or you could go around to other people yourself and subtly ask them their opinion about your performance. This might be a very difficult thing for you to do but may be a very important part of your improvement.

THE VALUE OF VIDEO

One of the greatest technological advances for therapy over recent years has been the increasing availability of good video equipment. Most people now have access to video recording and playing equipment, if not their own, then through a friend or rental agency. If you can get hold of a video camera and player, you can use them to great advantage in helping to obtain feedback about your social performances.

In the previous section we were talking about the value of getting feedback from other people. While this is a very important thing to do, most of us would put a lot more credence into information seen through our own eyes than via someone else. This is where a video camera can be very useful. Through the video camera you can get a chance to see how you really performed. Obviously, there are limitations in terms of when or where you can use a camera. You won't be able to get video feedback about things like meeting new people, telling jokes, or going on a first date. But you can easily get video feedback on more formal tasks like playing music at a recital, delivering a speech, or giving a business presentation. All you need to do is to have a reason ("I'd like to show my mother" or "I'd like to remember all the points we come up with") and then set up the equipment. Just as with your personal rater, you can use the video feedback to decide whether you are performing better than you think, or whether there are certain parts of your performance that you need to work on.

As an example, let me tell you about Tom, a young boy I treated several years ago. Tom was 15 and wanted to be a professional guitarist. He was a very good guitar player but unfortunately did not believe that he was. As a result, he was seriously thinking about giving it up. Tom's family and I told him that he was a very good player, but he simply thought that we were being nice. So I arranged for Tom to play in front of a small audience and then videoed the entire recital. I asked Tom to rate how he thought he had done. He rated himself very badly. In particular, he wrote that he was "shaking so much that he must have looked really stupid." We then looked at the video recording together. Before I said a word, Tom turned to me with a huge grin on his face and said, "I'm really good. I can't even see myself shaking."

Many people report that when they watch themselves on video they become very self-conscious. This is a common feeling for anyone. Unfortunately, there is no way to get around it except to just push on through. Remember Lesson 6 on reality testing: if you watch yourself several times, it will become easier. The most important point is to try not to become coy and pick faults with yourself such as "I don't like the way my hair looks." Rather, it is very important that you try to look at yourself like an outsider would. Try to pretend the person on the video is not you and look very objectively at how he performs. Having a set of points and behaviors to rate, just as we discussed earlier, will be very helpful. Finally, if you find you are really having trouble being objective, try to find a trusted other person to watch it with you (or alone if you can't bear to sit with him while he watches) and give you honest feedback.

IMPROVING YOUR PERFORMANCE

As we discussed earlier, when you get feedback, either from another person or a video recording, you may decide that there are parts of your performance that need some work. For example, you may decide you are not very smooth at introducing people to each other, or you may feel your public speaking skills are not very good. In this case it is often a good idea to work on these aspects to make a better impression on people and to build your general confidence.

The first and most important aspect of working on your performance is to get feedback based on clear, specific behaviors. It is much easier to improve your speaking ability, for example, if you have been told that you do not keep enough eye contact with the audience or your voice is not loud enough, than if you have simply been told that you do not speak well. Getting enough clear and specific detail about exactly what is lacking is the key.

Another useful technique is to watch other people, especially those who are good at performing and try to model yourself on them. Again, specifics is the key. It is much harder to say "I want to be like her" than to say, "One of the best things about her performance is that her voice is loud and clear." Try to observe a number of people doing the activities you would like to do and make note of exactly what sorts of things they do or do not do that seem to make their performance so good.

Finally, probably the most useful technique of all is the use of role play. Role playing simply means acting or pretending to be in a particular situation without actually being there. Once again, you will need to enlist the aid of honest, trustworthy friends. For example, you might decide you want to ask the boss for a raise. You might get

85

one friend to play the part of the boss and then you will act out exactly how you would approach him. Your friend could give you clear feedback about how your request came across. This is also a good opportunity to use video. Once you have the feedback, you can again try working on improving the behaviors that weren't so strong. You can then get some more feedback and try again, and so on. By the time you come to really approach your boss, your anxiety will be much less, both because you know you will do a better job of it and because you will have practiced it several times.

BUILDING CONFIDENCE IN SOCIAL GROUPS: GEORGE'S EXAMPLE

Do you remember George from our introduction? He had been a loner for much of his life and had very little practice meeting and interacting with other people. Getting feedback and learning how to interact better with others was therefore very important to him. Luckily, George was seeing a therapist to help overcome his social phobia. The therapist was able to provide a lot of feedback to George and help him to learn to deal with people better.

To begin with, the therapist set up a meeting situation. With George's permission, the therapist invited a colleague of his into the session. George was told to pretend that he had gone to the laundromat to wash his clothes and that there was only one other person there (the colleague). His task was to try to engage the other person in a conversation and talk to him for up to ten minutes while the therapist videoed the entire interaction.

Following the role play, the therapist asked George how he thought he had done. George looked very miserable and said that he thought he was "completely hopeless. I must have sounded so stupid—I just mumbled garbage and couldn't think of anything to say."

In fact, George's performance, while not perfect, had not been too bad. The first step was for the therapist to feed this back to him in the most convincing way possible. The therapist played the video of the interaction to George and told him to pretend that he was looking at someone else and to rate all of the good and bad points. After watching the video, George was able to see that there were certainly some things to work on, but that overall, it hadn't been a total disaster.

Next, the therapist and George sat down to discuss the good and bad aspects of George's performance. Both agreed that George had managed to find a few interesting topics to ask the other person about, that he had sat in a way that helped to make the other person feel comfortable, and that he had listened very attentively when the other person spoke. Then they discussed some of the main things that George needed to work on. These were as follows: (1) he needed to maintain more direct eye contact when he spoke; (2) he needed to speak a little more slowly, loudly, and clearly; and (3) he needed to put a little more expression into his voice and more movement into his body. Finally, George himself raised the problem that he felt as though he couldn't think of anything to talk about and he needed a better range of conversation topics. The therapist and George then went through each of these problems. They discussed each one, spoke about the specifics of what George was doing wrong, explored examples of good and bad ways of acting, and then practiced these examples together so that George could really see what he was doing. Then the therapist and George went through a few longer role plays so that George could practice all of the behaviors together while the therapist gave feedback. Finally, the therapist invited his colleague back in and George repeated the laundromat role play, which was again videoed. George was then able to compare his earlier performance with this later one and was pleased to see how much he had improved.

SUMMARY

In this lesson you learned about the importance of feedback about how you come across in social situations.

- In many cases you will find that your performance is actually better than you think it is. Feedback can help to prove this to you.

- In other cases, there will be aspects of your performance that you need to work on. Feedback can help to tell you exactly what you need to change.

- To get feedback in situations you will need to be clever. Try to let your mind go to think of all sorts of different ways in which you might get some honest feedback about your performance in various situations. The best method is to rely on another person whom you trust to be honest, yet caring. However, there are other ways that you might come up with if you let your imagination go.

- If possible, try to video some of your performances. This is the best way to get feedback for yourself.

- If you discover that you need to work on some parts of your performance, try to get very clear and specific points to follow.

- Then try to practice these new behaviors with someone by doing role play.

88

TASKS AND CHECKLIST

Your task for this lesson is to begin to get feedback and improve your performance in social situations.

✓ Try to come up with several situations in which you do not feel you perform very well and write them down. Some of them may come from your Reality Testing Stepladders.

✓ Think about how you might get some feedback about your performance in these situations. Can you get a trusted friend to watch you? Can you video yourself in some way?

✓ Select one or two of these performances and arrange to do them and get feedback in the coming week.

✓ Where your feedback shows that you could improve your performance, arrange to do some role play and practice doing your performance in new and better ways.

✓ Continue to do your Reality Testing and keep recording your practices.

✗ You can stop doing formal practice of your Attention Training if you wish, but it is not a bad idea to keep practicing, at least a few times per week.

TAKING STOCK

By now you have been going through the program for several weeks, either by yourself or preferably with a therapist. You should be familiar with each of the techniques and you should be noticing positive changes in your levels of confidence and social anxiety. This is probably a good point to sit down and take stock of where you are and where you want to head from here.

PUTTING IT ALL TOGETHER

Until now we have discussed each of the techniques almost as separate, independent components. This was never the real intention and I hope you have been able to combine techniques yourself as needed. However, now that we have explained and practiced each of the techniques, it may be a good time to go over how they should all be used in combination.

The basic cornerstone of this program is realistic thinking. It is very important to practice, practice, practice this technique and to get to the point where your fundamental beliefs about social situations begin to change. This should already be starting to happen for you. Remember that the attitude you should be able to get to is "People probably are not thinking badly of me and, even if they are, it doesn't really matter." You need to back up your realistic thinking with reality testing. These two techniques together will help to give you the attitudes mentioned above. Combining these two techniques is the most powerful way to change your beliefs: first, thinking through the situation realistically and looking for evidence for your beliefs, and second, going ahead and entering the situation to prove to yourself that nothing really bad will happen and to provide for yourself some more realistic evidence. Remember to look out for subtle ways of avoidance and to make sure you eliminate them. At this point, you should find that many situations that used to be quite frightening for you no longer cause nearly as much distress. Third, when you are in a situation and find yourself beginning to focus on your negative thoughts or on how you look, you need to shift your focus of attention to the task at hand. The practice you do at home on attentional training will help give you the ability to do this. Therefore, these three techniques—looking for realistic evidence for your beliefs, confronting your feared situations, and focusing attention on the task at hand—combine easily to help you feel confident and relaxed in social situations. Finally, you can embellish these procedures by using feedback from trusted others and video recordings and by doing regular role play to help practice your skills and build your confidence.

CONTINUING YOUR PRACTICE

Throughout this program I have tried to emphasize the importance of regular practice. The skills and techniques you need to overcome your shyness will not happen by magic. You need to practice them over and over and to apply them regularly in difficult situations. As you become better at these skills, you can begin to reduce your practice slightly so that it does not become so much of a chore. However, it is very important that you do not stop practice altogether. As you begin to improve, it is very easy to start thinking you are finished. But if you do, it will not take much for you to slip back to old ways. As you practice and improve, the techniques and attitude changes should start to become an automatic part of your life. As such, you should be able to keep practicing them without much effort as you go through your daily routine. The important thing is not to slip into a comfort zone where you no longer challenge yourself with difficult situations. If you find that you are doing this, don't forget about the motivational techniques we discussed in Lesson 1. Put some of them into play and get back to setting yourself goals and challenges. It is also a good idea to look back over your monitoring forms from time to time and see what you have accomplished. This can really help to boost your motivation by reminding you how far you have come and can also point out what areas may still need some work.

The ultimate rule is this: when you notice yourself avoiding a situation (or part of a situation), put your techniques into practice and force yourself to confront your fear. To fully overcome your shyness, confronting your fears should become your life's motto.

THE POSSIBILITY OF RELAPSE

We all like to think that when we have mastered something, it will stay with us forever. To some extent this is true. Once you begin to overcome your shyness, there will be many changes that you will make, both within yourself and in your life, that can never be taken away. However, it is also foolish to think that you can just sit back and your shyness will never return. Relapses can, and do, happen.

There are three possible reasons why you might notice your fears in social situations returning.

1. It is possible that a return of fear is not actually a relapse but is simply part of a temporary increase in anxiety in general. This is most likely to happen when you are under general pressure or stress, perhaps from work or from demands in your personal life. In this case, you would notice that you are feeling generally

stressed and tense and the increase in shyness may be just part of an overall, but temporary, loss of confidence. If this occurs, it is not a bad idea to begin to practice some of the techniques you have learned in this program again, just to make sure that your fears do not return and develop a life of their own. However, it is very likely that once you master your general life stressors, your overall confidence will return and your shyness will once again disappear.

2. Another common possibility is that your shyness and social fears will begin to return in a very subtle and gradual way over a long period. This is most likely to happen if you stop practicing your techniques and begin to take your confidence for granted. The return of fear in this way is usually very gradual and you may not notice it until you suddenly find that your life is beginning to become restricted again. This is not a major problem. It simply means that you need to go back to basics again for a few weeks and practice the techniques that you have learned. You will find that you can overcome these fears and get back to the level you were at much quicker the second time around. Of course, as we discussed earlier, it is much better to avoid this happening in the first place by continuing small amounts of practice for a number of years.

3. Finally, it is possible that you may notice a sudden and dramatic return of fear after a major upheaval or tragedy in your life. For example, if a person very close to you dies, you lose your job, or a serious relationship breaks up, it is very likely that you will suffer a major loss of confidence and, together with this, you will find your shyness returning. If this does occur, it is very important not to add any extra burden to yourself by becoming depressed over the return of your shyness. You need to remind yourself that when a major life event occurs, it is *natural* to lose some confidence. Time will be an important healer and you should probably just accept the shyness for a while and put your energies into

coping with the major event. Once it is behind you, you can then begin to work on the shyness. Again, this can be very easily done by going back to basics and starting the entire program from the beginning. You will find that things will happen much faster the second time and it will not take you very long to once again get on top of your social fears.

CHECKLIST FOR FUTURE PRACTICE

✓ Continue to practice and record Reality Testing, gradually working through all of your stepladders until you reach your most difficult tasks. This may take anywhere from a few weeks to a year or more depending on how hard you push yourself, how extensive your stepladders are, and the opportunities that arise.

✓ Even though you no longer need to be practicing your Realistic Thinking in a formal way, you should still use it whenever you do Reality Testing and return to formal practice and recording any time you find you are having difficulty with it. From time to time it does not hurt to return to formal practice and recording of Realistic Thinking for a week or so just to keep on top of it.

✓ Continue to get feedback on any activities where you feel that you tend not to perform well, and practice them whenever possible through role play or by actually doing them.

✓ You no longer need to do frequent, formal practice of your attention strengthening exercises as long as you feel able to focus your attention on whatever you are doing in social situations. However, it is not a bad idea to keep doing occasional practice (perhaps two or three times per week) just to keep your attention "fit." In addition, you should return to daily practice any time you find you are beginning to have difficulty keeping your attention focused.

✓ Remember to use the skills you have learned in this program to keep on top of your shyness. When you have a major event approaching or notice that you are starting to avoid certain events, do the following:

- Apply realistic thinking to the situation or activity.
- Practice the activity and get feedback.
- Construct a small stepladder and practice doing similar activities.
- Finally, do the activity and make sure you focus attention on the task at hand.

SPECIAL TOPICS

The situations that are frightening to people with social anxiety are many and varied. The basic principles that we have covered in this shyness program will help you to become confident in a wide variety of situations. You should already notice your confidence increasing, and continued practice, as we discussed in the previous lesson, will further these gains. For most people the program as we have covered it to this point is all they need to master their shyness and social phobia. However, there are three broad types of problems that are common sources of difficulty for many shy people and that might require some special effort if they present problems for you. These areas are: being unassertive, procrastinating or being perfectionistic, and having trouble trusting people. The techniques we have discussed to this point are the same ones that can be used to deal with these special problem areas. However, because these areas are often major sources of difficulty, we will spend a little time briefly discussing each one and looking at how your techniques can be applied to them.

BECOMING ASSERTIVE

People who are shy often also have difficulty in being assertive. This is often a source of serious distress. Being unassertive can sometimes lead to further anxiety and even depression.

Being assertive means being able to express your own needs while at the same time acknowledging the needs of others. An example might be asking a favor of others while at the same time accepting that they have a right to refuse and not feeling hurt or angry if they do. This is in contrast to two other behaviors: aggression and unassertiveness. When you are aggressive, you tend to put your own needs ahead of the needs of others (e.g., demanding a favor of someone and not accepting a refusal). When you are unassertive, you tend to put other people's needs ahead of your own (e.g., not asking a favor of someone for fear that you are imposing or will be refused).

Therefore, being assertive does not necessarily mean that you will get your way. Rather, it means feeling comfortable expressing your needs and letting others know what you want, while at the same time recognizing that other people also have needs that may be just as pressing as yours. In contrast to being aggressive, it means that sometimes your needs must give way to those of other people if theirs are more urgent. However, in contrast to being unassertive, it means that you should feel free to express your needs and that you can often expect your needs to be met, or at least to achieve a compromise. Examples of some assertive, aggressive, and unassertive statements are given in Table 9–1.

Why Are You Unassertive?

Shy people are very rarely aggressive. However, they often have problems because they are too unassertive. There are two main reasons shy people may be unassertive. First, some people simply do not know how best to express their needs. They just do not have the skills or the language to get their way successfully. If this is true for you, you will need to learn different ways of expressing yourself to help you get your needs across clearly to the other person, while at

Table 9–1. Examples of assertive, aggressive, and unassertive behavior

Situation	Unassertive Response	Aggressive Response	Assertive Reponse
Being asked a favor that is not possible	I guess I can try to fit it in	You've got to be kidding	I realize it is important for you, but I'm afraid my time is full up today
Wanting to ask a favor that is not very pleasant	Avoidance, i.e., don't ask	I want you to do something for me	It would really help me a great deal if you would be able to do "x" for me
Reacting to an inconvenience	I guess I'll just live with it	Stop that right now	I would really prefer it if you could move elsewhere to do that

the same time letting her know that you understand and respect her position. We do not have space in this book to go through this type of training in great detail, but I will briefly describe some techniques below.

The second main reason people may be unassertive is a consequence of social anxiety. In this case you might know how to be assertive but you just don't do it. This is usually because you are too shy or frightened to say what you want. To change this pattern, you need to apply the skills and techniques that you have learned in this shyness program to the specific problem of unassertiveness. I will discuss how to do this shortly.

Assertive Language

As already mentioned, the first step is to learn exactly how best to get across your assertive message. The idea is to express your needs while at the same time letting the other person know that you respect his needs. If you are not sure of how you are coming across to the other person, it is often a good idea to put yourself mentally in his position (remember your Realistic Thinking). Ask yourself, "If he said this to me, how would I feel?" If you think that you would feel angry or hurt, then you are obviously not expressing yourself well. But if you think that you would be okay about what you are going to say, there is no reason you should not say it. Here are some very simple rules to follow.

Watch Your Nonverbals

Your message will more likely be heard and listened to if you present a confident and clear picture. Good eye contact, an upright, relaxed posture, and a clear voice give the image of someone who knows what he wants and is confident of getting it. When you look at the ground, shuffle your feet, or mumble, you give the impression that you are shifty, that you are not sure that you really want what you are asking for, and that you expect to be refused. On the other hand, you also need to make sure that you don't come across as too overbearing. Make sure you don't stand too close, don't stare, and definitely keep your voice calm and level. Yelling only makes people defensive.

Be Empathetic

Remember, being assertive involves acknowledging that the other person in the situation also has rights and that these are important. When you make an assertive comment, you are much more likely to be listened to if you let the other person know that you recognize her side of the situation. For example, consider the following two statements: "I want you to stay back and finish this paperwork" or "I realize that you want to get home, but I need you to stay back and finish this paperwork." In the second statement, you are letting the person know that you understand your request will cause an inconvenience. By acknowledging this, you are telling the person that her needs are of concern to you, but that you consider your needs more urgent at this time.

Use "I" Statements
"I" statements talk about yourself when you say something, instead of talking in generalities. In other words, you should own your feelings. This is particularly important when you are expressing negative ones. Consider the following two statements: "People have trouble breathing when you smoke in here" or "My breathing is irritated when you smoke in here." The first statement leaves you open to argument and resentment. You might get the response, "What do you know about people's breathing?" With the second statement, there is no possibility for argument and it also shows that you are being open and honest.

Describe the Causes and Effects
Letting people know the entire situation rather than simply making a demand is much more likely to convince them that your rights and desires are important. In particular, when you want people to change something, it is very useful to tell them exactly what it is that you want changed and why. For example, consider the following two demands: "Will you stop talking!" or "When you talk, it is hard for me to hear the film." The second version clearly indicates the behavior you are not happy with and its effect on you and is much more likely to be complied with and less likely to cause offense.

Suggest an Alternative
Following from the above rule, making a suggestion to people about alternative behavior that would be acceptable to you will further help to defuse the situation. For example, something like the following would be good. "When you talk, it is hard for me to hear the film. Perhaps you could chat in the next room." By making a rea-

sonable suggestion to people about how they could change, you are letting them know that you accept their right to do what they are doing and suggesting that you are trying to find a mutually satisfactory solution.

Dealing with Aggression

At times, no matter how careful you are in your assertiveness, you will find other people becoming aggressive toward you. This can be very distressing. Here are a couple of suggestions for trying to minimize or combat aggression.

Don't Buy In

The main rule with aggression is not to buy into it and start being aggressive in return. When you are aggressive to someone who is angry, it will only serve to increase his anger, and the whole interaction can spiral out of control. It is even better to back off and try again at another time and place than to fuel the anger.

Keep Calm

The best way to defuse someone's anger is to stay calm and in control. If you have a spare few seconds while the other person is being angry, try using your Realistic Thinking to help you control your own feelings. Is the other person really better than you? Is the other person really going to hit you? Is the other person going to get his way? Does it matter if the other person doesn't like you? And so on. Once you are able to calm your feelings, try to follow through with your manner. It is very hard for someone to get carried away with aggression if you are looking him confidently in the eye, speaking in a gentle, quiet manner, and standing in a relaxed, non-aggressive posture.

Use "I" Statements

It is much harder for someone to argue with you and get angrier if you own your own feelings and don't make broad sweeping statements.

Be Empathetic

Similarly, it is hard to be angry at someone who seems to understand your side of the story. Rather than just trying to force your view on the other person, try beginning by acknowledging his perspective. You are then much more likely to get your message across successfully.

Point Out Assumptions

Sometimes someone's anger is based on unstated assumptions or misunderstandings. Rather than simply hearing what the person is saying to you at a superficial level, try to step back a little mentally and see the situation from his side. Try to understand the underlying assumptions behind the anger. If you realize that there is a misunderstanding or that you are talking at cross purposes, you can then feed that back to the person in a calm and objective manner.

Stick to Your Point

Finally, in some cases, it is just not possible to defuse the situation totally. In such instances, it is often useful to repeat your message over and over. Each time, you should begin by acknowledging what the other person is saying, but then simply go on and repeat your message. For example, "I would like to see the manager, please," "Yes, I realize that it's very late, but I really do need to see the manager," "I know you would like to get home, but it is important for me to see the manager," and so on. Obviously, if the situation looks as though it might become violent, or you are really going to get nowhere, it is always better to back off and try again at a later time when everyone has calmed down.

Letting Shyness Get in the Way

As I pointed out earlier, one of the main reasons shy people are often unassertive is that they let their shyness get in the way. They might have thoughts along the lines, "I'm not important enough," or "If I say that, then she will get angry and won't like me anymore," or perhaps, "If I say that, I will hurt her feelings." Perhaps you see some of these thoughts in yourself. Either way, I'm certain you can recognize them as typical of someone who is shy. In addition, you should be able to understand by now that these thoughts are probably unrealistic.

An assertiveness situation is often just another frightening social situation. By now, you should know exactly how to address it: (1) You need to challenge your thoughts in the situation and look for evidence for your extreme beliefs. You then need to have a look at the consequences of these beliefs by asking "So what?" One of the best sources of evidence for assertiveness is to put yourself in the other person's position. Imagine that he had just asked you the same favor or had just said no to the same request. How would you feel about him? (2) You need to reality test by getting yourself to perform assertive actions or make assertive comments and seeing for yourself exactly what happens. If some of these situations are too hard to begin with, you need to develop an assertiveness stepladder and gradually work your way up. Try to brainstorm a number of situations related to being assertive that you find difficult and place them on a stepladder in order of difficulty. (3) When you begin to act assertively, you need to focus your attention on what you are saying and what the other person is saying to you. Try to stop your attention from being dragged onto what the other person might be thinking of you or on how flushed and uncomfortable you might look. (4) You may want to help all this along by acting out the situation in

a role play with a trusted friend and getting feedback before embarking on the real thing.

Jenny's Example

Jenny felt that she had a lot of difficulty being assertive and decided that this was a very important issue to work on to help build her confidence. She began by asking her husband Jim to give her some feedback on how she generally acts in situations where she could be more assertive. Jim told her that in many cases where he felt she should say what she thinks, Jenny simply held her views and desires to herself. On some occasions, however, Jim told her that she seemed to try to be assertive, but came across as aggressive. At these times, Jenny could have benefited by giving people a better idea of the reasons she was asking for something and also using calmer and more relaxed nonverbal messages. So Jim and Jenny agreed to try some role play of different hypothetical assertive situations and Jim gave Jenny feedback on how she came across to him. In addition, they videoed these role plays so that Jenny could see for herself how she came across and could adjust her behavior accordingly.

After several sessions of role play, Jenny felt more confident in her ability to act assertively. The next step was to think of as many assertiveness situations as she could that made her feel shy and nervous. She then organized these into a stepladder. Jenny then imagined a few of these situations and used her Realistic Thinking Record to challenge her thoughts hypothetically and begin to think more realistically about being assertive with people. She also did this for a few major events from her past when she had been particularly unassertive. Finally, Jenny spent several weeks doing Reality Testing and gradually working her way up the stepladder. This was done both by setting up some situations intentionally (for example, she bought items from shops with the express intention of returning them) as well as grabbing natural opportunities when they arose. Part of Jenny's stepladder for assertiveness is shown below.

7. Talk to neighbor about his barking dog
6. Buy medium priced article from small store and return it
5. Buy medium priced article at large store and return it
4. Tell canteen manager that I can't go in to help one day
3. Ask family for small favors
2. Refuse to give a ride home to Susan from canteen
1. Refuse simple requests from family (e.g., rides, errands)

PERFECTIONISM AND PROCRASTINATION

You have an assignment due. You sit down to begin writing, but you can't find just the right words. You may write a sentence, then tear it up, write another, and tear it up again. Then you remember that the oven needs cleaning and you rush off to do that and spend the rest of the afternoon doing odd jobs instead of writing your assignment. Sound familiar? Well, that's hardly surprising. The two P's, *perfectionism* and *procrastination*, are a common feature of socially anxious people. Just like unassertiveness, they are simply another form of social fear. Shy people often say that they become perfectionistic in what they do because they are worried about what others will think of them if they make a mistake. For example, "What will the neighbors think if my front lawn isn't mowed?" or "My boss will think I'm sloppy if I have any spelling errors in my work."

If you are perfectionistic about doing things, then it becomes a real strain to do them. As a result, it's not surprising when you put them off as much as you can. After all, it's much easier to avoid doing work altogether than to face the stress of trying to get it absolutely right.

It is easy to see that perfectionism can be thought of simply as a type of social avoidance: avoidance of the possibility of making a mistake or of doing a less-than-perfect job. In order to work efficiently, most people are willing to accept the probability that there are minor problems in their work. Obviously more important or

detailed work requires more checking, while less important work requires less checking. If you obsessively check and re-check your work all the time, then what you are doing is making absolutely sure—beyond a doubt—that there is nothing wrong with it. In other words, you are avoiding the possibility of making mistakes in your work. But in most cases, this is completely unnecessary. After all, the chances that you have made mistakes in your work (and missed them the first time you checked), are quite small. More important, even if you have made an error or two, it is usually not the end of the world. For example, your boss is hardly going to fire you just because you spelled a few words wrong! Therefore, in order for you to become more efficient in your work, it is important for you to learn that if you don't check your work frequently, the world does not fall apart.

It must be very obvious by now that the best techniques to help you combat your perfectionism (and similarly your procrastination) are the Realistic Thinking and Reality Testing. You need to draw up a stepladder of things about which you are perfectionistic and practice trying to do them faster and with less checking. You might even try to make a few mistakes on purpose, just to see what will happen. When you do each one, you need to work out your negative predictions and then look at the evidence for them. Don't forget the "so what" challenge as the most important part. It may be quite likely that you will make a small mistake, but is this really a tragedy? As for social situations, putting yourself in someone else's position is a very useful way to get some realistic perspective. For example, if your boss wrote a piece that was not beautifully constructed, would you think that she was incompetent?

Heather's Example

Part of Heather's problem involved a tendency to be overly perfectionistic. Heather hated making mistakes of any kind and always tried to make certain that everything she did and said was completely correct. As a result she often held back in conversations and it took a great deal of effort for her to start any task because she was always so worried that she would not do it well enough. Recently, Heather's perfectionism and procrastination had become serious problems for her. She had finally found work as secretary to a manager in an insurance company. However, her work was very slow because she was continually checking it, and it was a real struggle for her to begin new tasks.

Heather's first step was to complete her Realistic Thinking Record for several instances at work and at home where she became worried about the possibility of making mistakes. In every instance, Heather quickly realized that she was much more unlikely to make mistakes than she thought and that even if she did, it was never going to be as bad as she imagined. One of Heather's Realistic Thinking examples is shown in Table 9–2.

Next, Heather thought about a number of events and situations having to do with making mistakes that made her anxious, and she placed these into a stepladder in order of difficulty. Heather then worked her way up the stepladder. As one of her tasks, she was typing a letter for her boss and she intentionally made three small spelling mistakes. She held her breath while her boss read over the letter. To her amazement, he simply handed back the letter, pointed out two of the errors (he missed one himself), and asked her to fix them before sending it out. There was no explosion, no criticism, and he certainly did not fire her. Part of Heather's stepladder is shown on p. 110.

It is important to acknowledge that for someone who is perfectionistic, deliberately making mistakes will be very difficult. This is true of all reality testing tasks. By definition, reality testing is difficult because you are forcing yourself to do precisely those things that you have spent your energy trying to avoid. Nevertheless, you need to remind yourself that if you continue to avoid, you will not improve. Only by doing those things that you find difficult will you learn that they are not as bad as you thought. Remember that if a task is too difficult for you, you can make it easier by breaking it down into smaller steps and working your way up the ladder more gradually.

Table 9–2. One of Heather's Realistic Thinking samples regarding making mistakes

Event	Expectation (Initial Prediction)	Evidence (How do I know)	Probability (Realistic)	Degree of Emotion (0–8)	Consequences (What if)
Make a typing mistake on letter	The boss will think I am incompetent.	I have rarely made mistakes before. I have never had any indication till now that the boss thinks I am incompetent. Other secretaries make mistakes and they are not thought incompetent. I wouldn't think the boss was incompetent if he made a mistake.	Quite low	3	I will lose my job.
	I will lose my job.	If I thought someone was incompetent after one instance, I would give her another chance. Making one typing mistake is not enough to lose my job over.	Low	2	I will never find another.
	I will never find another.	I found this job quite easily. I am generally a careful and good worker.	Low	1	

Degree of emotion

0	1	2	3	4	5	6	7	8
none		slight		moderate		quite a bit		extreme

7. Call brother-in-law day after birthday instead of on correct day
6. Intentionally make several typing errors in letter
5. Underpay telephone account by a few dollars
4. Intentionally make one typing error in letter
3. Check important reports only once after typing
2. Place file in wrong section
1. Check unimportant letters only once after typing

Note: It is important to point out that the idea of Reality Testing was not to make Heather sloppy, but to help her realize that an occasional mistake is not an absolute tragedy and, in this way, to reduce her concern about always being perfect.

DEVELOPING TRUST

For most of us, life involves a series of relationships with other people. If each of these relationships is going to succeed, there must be mutual trust. This trust obviously involves a degree of risk. It is easy for someone we care about to hurt us badly. But most of us take these risks with pleasure because of the huge benefits of a satisfying relationship. If we do get hurt, we need to try to understand the motivations involved, deal with the hurt feelings, and perhaps try to assess the situation realistically. Then, in most cases, we try again.

Most socially phobic people do not have great difficulty developing satisfying, trusting relationships. However, there is a small group, usually with more severe symptoms, who are very wary of other people and who, as a result, develop few if any close relationships with others. If you are one of these people, then you may want to work on this aspect of your personality so that you can expand on a potentially wonderful part of human life. Working on a lack of basic trust is not an easy thing and usually requires a long and slow program. However, the results are well worth it.

A trust-building program could easily be another entire book. Here, however, I can briefly describe some of the principles in terms of the techniques we have already covered. If you are a person who lacks basic trust in other people, then you really need to be working on this with a therapist. Trust is not a simple or an easily accomplished characteristic to develop and the care and guidance of a good therapist will be invaluable in helping you along the way.

The first step is to treat your lack of trust as another type of social avoidance. There are probably many forms of subtle avoidance involved here. For example, you may not divulge anything personal about yourself at work or in groups, you may avoid getting close to a potential romantic partner, or you may never ask anyone to do you a favor. You need to think carefully about the subtle ways in which you avoid getting close to people and then try to work out a stepladder of tasks you could try. Remember that these types of reality tests are not easy and you should take small steps. Don't push yourself too hard, but be patient. As usual, with each reality test you need to pay attention to your attitudes and beliefs in the situation and carefully examine the evidence to work out what is realistic and what is not. It is very easy for some people to misinterpret very innocent actions from others and believe that these other people are intentionally trying to hurt them. For example, I was treating a young girl of 15 who had a difficult time with a boy at a social function. The girl had said hello to the boy and he had taken one look at her and had turned around and walked away. My client saw this as an example of the "fact" that everyone hated her and people intentionally tried to avoid her. However, when we looked carefully at whether there were other possible explanations for the boy's actions, she realized that the boy may have had other things on his mind, that he may have had a bad day, or that he himself may have been shy. When you are doing your reality testing and opening yourself up to trust situations, it is very important to remind yourself that people are not likely to want to intentionally hurt you and that hurts or insults you do experience may occur for all sorts of innocent reasons. Checking out these possible reasons where possible, such as actually asking the person or someone else who is there, can often help keep you from jumping to false conclusions.

In building trust, it is also often a good idea to think about where your original lack of trust may have come from. Being able to discuss these issues in detail, either with a therapist or a trusted friend, can be very valuable. It may be that you were badly hurt earlier in your life. For example, you may have been physically, sexually, or emotionally abused as a child or you may have been abandoned by a trusted person. On the other hand, you may have copied these attitudes from an important figure in your life. The actual event is not as important as it is to get an understanding of where your attitudes may have come from and how they have helped to shape your life. This can sometimes help to convince you of the unrealistic nature of these beliefs or at least make it easier to give them up to some degree.

George's Example

George had difficulty trusting people for as long as he could remember. Whenever someone smiled at him or began to appear interested in him, George would immediately assume the person wanted something and he would back away.

In discussing his early life with his therapist (something George found very hard to do), he realized that many of his feelings came from his relationship with his father. George's father had been an alcoholic who had constantly belittled and criticized him, often in front of other people. At the same time, his father had pushed him to work extremely hard and "make something" of his life. George found that he was always trying to please his father, which usually involved a very careful approach because he never knew what sort of mood his father would be in. Finally, when George was 12, his father shot himself. In therapy, George realized that he had never been able to please his father. These insights did not suddenly make him begin trusting people—that would be a long, slow road—but they did help him understand where he came from and why he thought the way he did. In addition, they helped him decide that he did not need to be like that and that he would try harder than ever to change his ways of thinking.

George and his therapist then worked out a detailed stepladder for him to follow. The steps of the ladder were very small and he was to take them slowly. Before each step, the therapist and George discussed George's beliefs about the situation and looked at the realistic evidence for them. A list of some of the items from George's stepladder follows.

---

8. Reveal to boss that you sometimes get nervous in certain situations.
7. Invite neighbor to a movie that you choose.
6. Give a difficult, personally revealing opinion to boss (e.g., on politics).
5. Invite neighbor into home for a drink.
4. Give a moderately revealing opinion to boss (e.g., on football).
3. Give a simple, non-revealing opinion to boss (e.g., on the weather).
2. Smile at a female stranger on the street.
1. Smile at a male stranger on the street.

CONCLUSION AND A WORD ABOUT DRUGS AND ALCOHOL

Congratulations! If you have been following this program through and doing all of the exercises along the way, it has been a long, hard road to get here but it has been well worth it. By now, you should be feeling far more confident and comfortable in social situations than you were when you started this program. If you are not sure, look back through your Social Situations Record from the beginning of the program and remind yourself of the extent of your shyness back then. As your confidence builds, it is easy to forget what you were like even a few weeks ago. If you have continued to use your Social Situations Record throughout the program then you will have a good record of how you have progressed over the past few months.

Your change is not complete, nor will it probably ever be. As you will recall, social phobia is partly caused by genetics and also partly by your early life experiences. Therefore, overcoming shyness is not something that is very likely to be finished in any absolute sense. Rather, we hope the techniques and procedures you have learned have become a part of your life, your new way of dealing with the world. If so, you will continue to keep overcoming your shyness for the rest of your life. This shouldn't be seen as a burden but as an opportunity for continued growth.

Before ending, I need to discuss the issue of drugs briefly. If drugs were a part of how you coped with your social phobia in the past, you will need to think about eliminating them from your life. By now, you should have enough confidence so that you really do not need drugs any more to help get you through social situations. If you are taking medication that was prescribed by a doctor, you need to go back to that doctor and ask him or her to help you stop taking the medication. Describe the program you have been working and explain to the doctor that you now feel confident to come off the medication. You should never simply stop taking medication yourself. Rather, any long-term medication you were on needs to be eased off gradually and your doctor will be able to tell you exactly how. If all of this program has been done while you were on a particular medication, you will need to make sure that you go through all of your Reality Testing again, this time when you are off the medication. Don't be too disappointed if you find it difficult to face some situations again. This is only natural. The way to overcome it is once again through practice. Try incorporating your medication reduction into your stepladder. For example, you might say hello to someone on the bus at first on your full dose of medication, then a second time on three-quarters of your medication, a third time on half your medication, and so on.

If you have been drinking alcohol or taking medication on a casual basis to get you through particular social situations, you need to make sure that facing these situations without your drug is incorporated into your stepladder. People who are on regular medication should repeat each step on gradually lower doses of the drug. If you find you are having a lot of difficulty cutting out your alcohol or medication, you should see a mental health practitioner.

I hope your friends and relatives have begun to notice a more confident you and that your life has lost many of the restrictions it once had. Our friends Adam, Jenny, Heather, and George all made great changes in their lives. I hope you have been able to as well and wish you every success with your future.

INDEX

Aggression, assertiveness and, 102–105

Alcohol, 115–116

Alternatives, assertiveness and, 101

Assertiveness, 98–105
  aggression and, 102–105
  example, 105–106
  language and, 99–102
  unassertiveness, causes of, 98–100

Attention training, 53–61
  exercises for, 55–57, 58
  overview, 53–55
  practice in, 57, 59–60
  tasks and checklist, 61

Automatic thoughts, realistic thinking, 25

Avoidance, reality testing, 68–69

Basic beliefs. *See* Beliefs

Behavioral system, shyness effects, 19

Beliefs
  challenging of, 46, 50–51
  realistic thinking, 49–50

Cause and effect, assertiveness and, 101

Change process, motivation and self control, 2, 3

Confidence, in social groups, feedback, 86–87

Consequences of errors, realistic thinking, 40–41

Drugs, 115–116

Emotions, realistic thinking, 24

Empathy, assertiveness and, 100–101

Environment, shyness and, 14–16

Experience
  realistic thinking, probability estimation, 29–30
  shyness and, 16

Family patterns, shyness and, 15

Fear identification, record keeping, 5

Feedback, 79–89
    overview, 79–81
    performance improvements,
        85–86
    social group confidence, 86–
        87
    sources of, 81–83
    tasks and checklist, 89
    video camera, 83–85
Feelings, realistic thinking, 24
Financial rewards, motivation
        and self control, 3–4

Genetics, shyness and, 13–
        14

"I" statements
    aggression and, 103
    assertiveness and, 101

Language, assertiveness and,
        99–102
Learning skills, record keeping,
        5
Life experience. See Experience

Medication, 115–116
Meditation, attention training, 59
Mental system, shyness effects,
        16–17
Mini-meditations, attention
        training, 59
Mood, reality testing and,
        67–68

Motivation and self control, 1–10
    change process, 2, 3
    definitions, 2–4
    overview, 1–2
    record keeping, 4–9
    tasks and checklist, 10

Nonverbal language, assertive-
    ness and, 100

Objectivity, record keeping, 5

Perfectionism and procrastina-
        tion, 106–110
    example, 107–110
    overview, 106–107
Performance improvements,
        feedback, 85–86
Physical system, shyness
        effects, 17–18
Positive thinking, realistic
        thinking contrasted, 25
Probability estimation, realistic
        thinking, 29–33
Procrastination. See
        Perfectionism and pro-
        crastination
Punishment methods, motiva-
        tion and self control, 3–4

Rapee, R. M., xv
Realistic thinking, 23–52. See
        also Unrealistic thinking
    beliefs, 49–50
    consequences of errors, 40–41

examples, 41–48
  of others, 41–43
  of self, 43–48
  extremes and, 24–25
  overview, 23–24
  probability estimation,
    29–33
  record keeping, 33–37
  shyness and, 25–26
  tasks and checklist, 38, 52
  thinking errors, 39
  thought identification,
    26–28
Reality testing, 63–77
  avoidance, 68–69
  future practice, checklist for,
    95–96
  initiation of, 73–74
  mood and, 67–68
  overview, 63–65
  practice of, 70–72
  record keeping, 74–75
  repetition, 67
  situational factors, 66–67
  step-by-step approach,
    65–66
  stepladder approach
    described, 69–70
    examples of, 72–73
  tasks and checklist, 77
Record keeping
  motivation and self control,
    2, 3, 4–9
  realistic thinking, 33–37, 47

reality testing, 74–75
treatment program, 19–20
Relapse, possibility of, 93–
  95
Repetition, reality testing, 67
Role reversal, realistic thinking,
    probability estimation,
    30–32

Sanderson, W. C., xv
Self-consciousness, video cam-
    era, feedback, 84
Self control. See Motivation
    and self control
Shyness
  age differences, 12–13
  aggression and, 102–104
  case examples, xi–xv
  causes of, 13–16
    environment, 14–16
    genetic, 13–14
  defined, x–xi
  effects of, 16–19
    behavioral system, 19
    mental system, 16–17
    physical system, 17–18
  gender differences, 12
  statistics on, 11–12
  treatment program, overview,
    19–20
  unrealistic thinking and,
    25–26
Situational factors, reality
    testing, 66–67

Social group confidence,
feedback, 86–87
Social phobia. *See* Shyness
Social rewards, motivation and
self control, 4
Social situations, record
keeping, 6–9, 22
Step-by-step approach, reality
testing, 65–66
Stock taking, 91–96

Thinking errors
consequences of, 40–41
realistic thinking, 39
Thinking realistically. *See*
Realistic thinking

Thought identification, realistic thinking, 26–28
Treatment program, overview,
19–20
Trust, 110–113
development of, 110–112
example, 112–113

Unassertiveness, causes of,
98–100
Unrealistic thinking. *See also*
Realistic thinking
identification of, 27–28
shyness and, 25–26

Video camera, feedback, 83–85

ABOUT THE AUTHOR

Ron Rapee received his Ph.D. in 1985 from University of New South Wales, Sydney, Australia and is currently Associate Professor in the Department of Psychology, Macquarie University, Sydney, Australia. Dr. Rapee has published extensively in international journals in the areas of child and adult anxiety and has written and edited several books.

CPSIA information can be obtained at www.ICGtesting.com
Printed in the USA
BVOW010426290911

272263BV00004B/4/P